How to Plan Your WESTERN BIG GAME HUNT

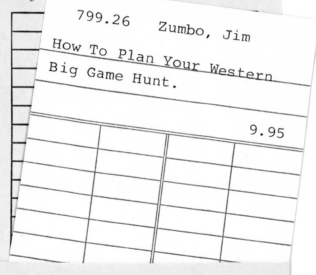

799.26   Zumbo. Jim
How To Plan Your Western
Big

799.26   Zumbo, Jim

How To Plan Your Western
Big Game Hunt.

9.95

D1017708

How to Plan Your
WESTERN
BIG GAME HUNT

Jim Zumbo

Stackpole Books

Published by
STACKPOLE BOOKS
Cameron and Kelker Streets
P.O. Box 1831
Harrisburg, PA 17105

Maps drawn by Carolyn Z. Roth

Printed in the U.S.A.

Library of Congress Cataloging-in-Publication Data

Zumbo, Jim.
    How to plan your western big game hunt.

    1. Big game hunting – West (U.S.) I. Title.
SK45.Z86 1986   799.2'6'0978   85-27670
ISBN 0-8117-2221-X

Contents

Introduction

The tidy deer camp was tucked into a small patch of quaking aspens. Firelight reflected eerie shadows on light-barked trees as the four hunters relaxed and stared into the crackling campfire. Back in the aspens, four mule deer bucks hung from a pole, cooling in the breezy night air.

While hunting earlier in the day, I met the men as they struggled to move two bucks from a pocket of thick timber to camp. I pitched in and helped, and was invited to eat dinner with them. This was their last evening in the Colorado mountains; they'd be heading to their home state of Pennsylvania in the morning.

"This has been an unbelievable trip," said Joe Crazik as he filled coffee cups from a blackened pot. "We've wanted to hunt deer in the West for a dozen years, and we finally got it together. Wait till the guys back at the mill hear about our trip."

The other men agreed, and they made a pact to return the following autumn.

A few weeks later I shared a tent with Steve, a man from West Virginia. We were camped high in Montana's Anaconda Pintlar Wilderness, hunting elk with an outfitter.

"I just can't believe I'm here," Steve said one evening after he pitched a chunk of spruce into the stove and settled back on his cot. "It's like a dream come true."

I knew how Steve felt. My first western big game hunt occurred twenty-one years ago, and I've never forgotten the electric excitement of killing my first mule deer. After years of reading about big-antlered bucks, I owned one. But it wasn't just the big buck lying on the Utah hillside that impressed me. It was everything around me – the newly discovered aroma of fresh sagebrush, the raucous cries of handsome magpies, the awesome canyons and razor-backed ridges that punctuated the earth's surface in every direction. These were the things that I did not know – could not know – until I left my bootprints in this land that Zane Grey, Teddy Roosevelt, and countless others had enjoyed before me.

"Welcome to the West, Steve," I said while screwing down the lantern knob. "There's nothing like it."

The inside of the tent grew darker as the lantern light weakened. Finally, all was black. It was time for dreams of great bull elk and giant mule deer.

"If I never fire a shot," Steve said, "this trip will still be a success. Just being in these mountains is enough of a reward."

A big game hunt in the West is a fantasy of sportsmen everywhere. Even hunters from foreign lands journey to America's West for a shot at bull elk, mule deer, antelope, and other big game creatures.

Despite the wonderful hunting, many outdoorsmen who have never been west shrug a trip off because of the uncertainty and expense. Putting together a hunt 1,000 to 2,000 miles away is often too much for someone who has never been there and has no contacts.

But let's say you're determined to make the trip. You and your pals are tired of staring at the elk and mule deer heads on the wall of the sportsman's club. In a courageous mood, your group decides to make a western big game hunt.

Where do you start? Many questions must be answered. Plenty of planning is required to put together a hunt. The better the plan, the better your chances for an enjoyable hunt.

I wrote this book to help you plan your trip. I've tried to include as many details as possible, and I sincerely hope your western hunt will be an outstanding success.

Jim Zumbo
Cody, Wyoming

I

Getting Started

Three basic decisions must be made before you plan your western hunt.

What species will you hunt?
What state(s) will you hunt?
Will you hunt on your own or hire an outfitter?

To make a trip by yourself, without the help of a guide, you must have the ability to get into game country, locate game, and get your game out. These are the three essentials. Of lesser importance, you'll need to be able to tend to yourself, that is, set up camp, cook, clean up, keep warm.

The degree of difficulty for doing a hunt on your own depends largely on the animal you're after. If you're hunting antelope, for example, it's often possible to live in a motel, eat in restaurants, and hunt your quarry from a paved or well-graded road. That's the easy extreme. If, on the other hand, you're after elk, mountain goats, sheep, or other animals that dwell in remote mountainous regions, then you'll need plenty of gear, woods skills, and preparation to live in high elevational environments.

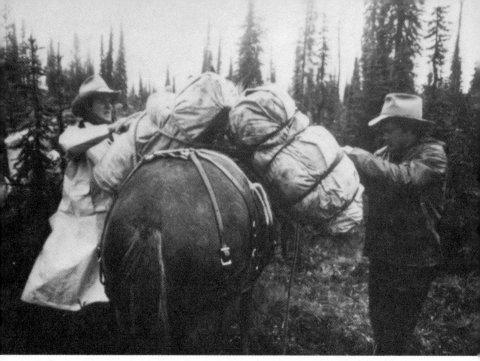

Packing gear in or out of hunting camp is a science. Outfitters have the know-how and will make the chore seem easy. These guides are packing elk meat out to a road from an Idaho backcountry camp.

An outfitter can eliminate many of the problems you encounter on a do-it-yourself hunt. He'll provide transportation into and out of the hunting area, guide you, feed you, give you a warm, dry place to sleep, and haul your game out of hunting country. If he's reputable and knows his terrain, he'll put you in good game country where your chances of seeing the kind of game you're interested in are optimal.

Since the expense of hiring an outfitter is an obvious drawback, you must carefully weigh the options. If you need to buy plenty of gear for your trip to make a hunt on your own, it may be cheaper in the long run to hire an outfitter. Also, you might make a number of do-it-yourself annual trips to the West without seeing or taking the kind of game you're hoping for. An outfitter could show you that game in a week to 10 days.

Determining the species to hunt is an easy decision, because most of us have favorites and know exactly what we want to hunt. It's possible, however, to do a combo hunt where two or more big game species can be hunted on the same trip, often in the same area. Mule deer and antelope are compatible combinations in some states, as are mule deer and elk. In some places, black bears are an added bonus that can be taken while hunting deer or elk.

When selecting the species, consider your resources before making plans. If you're going West for the first time, you may want to tackle antelope and/or mule deer on public land where you can make a relatively easy hunt. If you want an elk, consider how you'll get it out of the woods if you don't have horses. If you want a big-racked muley, figure on getting as far back in the hinterlands as you can, where hunting pressure is light because of difficult access. If you're equipped and are savvy about getting around western mountains, you can go after elk and muleys in remote regions.

Otherwise it's wise to consider hiring an outfitter or trying for animals that aren't of trophy status. There are plenty of modest 20- to 22-inch muleys running around in places relatively easy to hunt. Remember, too, that every state has so-called "quality units," or "limited-entry units." In many of these, access is good, hunting success is high, and you have a much better chance of taking a "difficult" species, such as elk, on those restricted hunts than on general hunts. Limited-entry unit tags are offered in a lottery. If you fail to draw, you get your money back, and you're out a bit of postage and perhaps a small application fee. If you draw, you have an opportunity for a species that you might otherwise be unable to hunt.

It's important to select a state that offers you the best opportunity for an animal. That might seem like poor advice, because every state in the Rockies offers mule deer and elk hunting, for example. Each state, however, offers different hunter success rates and varying odds at trophy-class animals. In addition, big game licenses are difficult to obtain in some states, easy in others. Combo hunts for two or more species may be offered in some states and not in others. (Consult Parts II and III of this book for specific information on big game species and the states in which to hunt them.)

As soon as possible, select those states which offer the kinds of hunts you want, and immediately send for big game hunting information. Application deadlines are well in advance of the hunting season. In Wyoming, for example, the traditional elk application deadline for nonresidents is February 1. In most of the best western states, nonresident big game tags are distributed via a lottery or a first-come, first-served system. It's vital to send your application and fee before the deadline — no excuses will help you if you miss it through ignorance or carelessness.

Have you been hunting a favorite western state with little or no success? Consider trying a new spot. Don't let a preference for a particular state deter you from exploring another. It may be unappealing to learn an unfamiliar area, but your luck might change. No two states are

alike. Hunting opportunities will differ according to big game management, weather, past winter mortality, hunter pressure, access, and other
factors. An astute hunter goes where his chances of scoring are best.

Outfitters—Do You Need Them?

Should you hire an outfitter? The decision to pay for his services
depends on a number of factors. There are advantages and disadvantages, with good arguments on each side.

Perhaps the most important advantage is access. Horses and mules
are necessary in transporting people and gear into remote regions. Without saddle and pack animals, the only choice is to hike and carry essential items on your back. That gets old in a hurry, particularly if you're
not in excellent physical condition and aren't capable of walking along
trails in the western mountains—most of which seem to be leading
uphill.

The trek to remote mountainous regions isn't made because outfitters like to lead folks fifteen or twenty miles into the outback. It's a fact
of life that some of the best big game hunting is in places difficult to
reach. Whether you want to pursue big-racked mule deer, elk, or trophy
sheep, your odds are often best in backcountry areas.

It's possible to rent horses and make a trip on your own, but be
advised that you'd better know how to pack. Unless you have the savvy
to tie the correct knots and load a horse or mule properly, forget a do-it-
yourself trip where pack animals are involved. Packing is a science; if
you haven't quite mastered it, you'll cuss the day you planned the trip.

Another reason to hire an outfitter is to take advantage of his knowledge. He'll know practically every trail in his territory, and he'll know
which high country regions produce game. He'll put you onto ridges and
basins that produce the best big game hunting, leaving the guesswork
out. That's not to say, of course, that your success is guaranteed. Too
many factors can influence a hunting trip. About all an outfitter can do
is try his best to make your experience a productive one.

You'll definitely appreciate an outfitter when it's time to transport
your animal *out* of the backcountry. His services almost always include
field-dressing, transporting the meat to camp, and hauling it out to your
vehicle or to a meat processor where you can make arrangements to
have it delivered to your home.

A mature bull elk will weigh 750 pounds to a half-ton on the hoof. If
you quarter a bull, which is standard procedure, you'll be hefting quarters that tip the scales at 90 pounds or more. And the chore of reducing
an elk to quarters is often a herculean task in itself. If you do it on your
own, be aware that you'll have earned the meat the hard way, and you

Horses are a hunter's best friend on a western hunt. They'll pack gear and meat and transport you to and from the hunting area. You don't need a horse when you hunt the West, but they're extremely helpful.

may never again make an attempt on an elk's life unless a road is handy or downhill, or both. You'll swear that the knives and saws intended for cutting up an elk were invented by sadists who enjoy human suffering, and you'll be convinced that an elk's bones are made of steel. The bottom line is it just ain't fun, or even possible, for some folks to move 400 or more pounds of meat through the mountain landscape, most of which will be designed to make the task as nasty as can be.

A final advantage in teaming up with an outfitter is having a bit of comfort around hunting camp. A cook will prepare and serve your meals, a wrangler or guide will tend to your horse, and you'll have a place to sleep. Tents, normally equipped with cots and woodstoves, will allow you to maintain some degree of protection from the elements, which can suddenly make life miserable. Autumn weather is fickle in the West. You can count on anything.

The obvious disadvantage to hiring an outfitter is the cost, but don't be surprised if the expense of a do-it-yourself trip closely matches that of a guided outing. By the time you buy the necessary gear, food, and figure transportation, your savings might be lower than anticipated. Currently, an outfitted hunt will cost $150 to $300 or more a day, depending on the game you're hunting, the length of the hunt, and other factors. A sheep hunt, for example, will be much more expensive than a deer or elk hunt. The fee usually covers pickup and return to a nearby airport, food, lodging, horses, and transportation of meat. You'll be expected to purchase your own hunting license and bring your own sleeping bag, firearm, ammo, and personal items.

If you want an economical outfitted hunt, consider a drop-camp. The outfitter will take you to an outback camp on horseback and drop you off for a prescribed period of time. Then he'll come back in and pack you and your game out. You'll be on your own while you're hunting, and you'll have the advantage of being in game country and having your animals packed out. This is an excellent compromise, and seems to be getting more popular each year.

There's also the risk of hiring a rogue outfitter. He isn't licensed, and he's apt to take you for a horseback ride or a cruise around the back roads, with no intention of showing you game.

How do you select an ethical outfitter? One way is to check the listings in the "where-to-go" sections of outdoor magazines, write to a number of outfitters, and request a list of references. Call the references rather than write; you'll learn much more on the phone. Another option is to meet with outfitters at the major sport shows held around the country to discuss their operations. A third is to work with a reliable booking agent. There's no charge for this service, and a good agent will be able to direct you to the outfitter best-equipped to meet your needs and expectations.

Another disadvantage to hunting with an outfitter, though one that can be easily resolved, is the necessity to keep up the pace set by your guide. Most western guides are young, tough cowboys who can walk and climb all day and make the effort seem like child's play. Unless you communicate to him the fact that you're not in the same league as he is, you'll have a rough time, and your hunt may well turn into an ordeal. Guides don't intentionally try to kill off their hunters – there's just plenty of ground to cover, and time is often of the essence when trying to reach prime game country.

Hunting on your own allows you to set your own speed and select your own hours. You can sleep as long as you want, and hunt according to your personal requirements. You can, of course, do the same on an outfitted trip, but you'll no doubt want to get the most out of the experience, which means sleeping little, hunting a lot, and feeling sorry for yourself when your out-of-shape body protests.

To some people, completing a project without professional assistance is important. These are folks who repair and maintain their own automobiles, or fix their plumbing leaks and electrical problems. Self-sufficient indoors as well as outdoors, they are willing to accept the hardships of doing it on their own, and realize a great deal of personal satisfaction by doing so. To them, hiring an outfitter is the easy way out. Whether you hire an outfitter depends on your personal requirements. You must determine your capability to make a backcountry trip, and decide whether you can afford the cost of a journey into remote mountains.

The Economy Hunt

The hunter with an eye on the budget can trim expenses and still have an enjoyable hunt. An ideal trip involves pooling two or three friends and driving west in an economy vehicle. If the vehicle is not meant for rugged use, it can still serve for transportation as long as you restrict travel to paved highway or graded secondary roads. Elk, deer, and antelope can be hunted from all-weather roads if the hunter is prepared to walk. It's also possible to rent a four-wheel drive vehicle in some towns, but there aren't that many of them available during hunting season.

You can eliminate camping expenses by staying at motels or boardinghouses close to hunting areas. By renting rooms with kitchenettes, you can cook your own meals and save money. Ski resorts and dude ranches welcome hunters, since many big game hunts occur during the off-season. It's possible to rent camp trailers and pickup campers, but demand will be high. You may have to place a reservation well in advance.

Forget about saving money on a nonresident big game license. Fees are high in all western states. Figure about $100 for a deer or antelope tag, $200 for elk, and more for sheep, goat, and moose.

If possible, plan a western family summer vacation in an area you'd like to hunt with your buddies in the fall. Besides looking over game country, you can talk to locals and get an idea about what to expect. You might even find a reasonably priced boardinghouse run by a little old lady whose son would just love to tell you where the good hunting spots are!

The Do-It-Yourself Hunt

First you must choose a state, then narrow your search to an area within it. If you're at square one and have no idea which state to hunt, read about your favorite species and where they're likely to be found in

Parts II and III of this book. It's also a good idea to read big game editions of outdoor magazines. Published in late summer each year, they report on hunting prospects in each state, along with the best places to go, regulations, seasons, fees, and application procedures. Don't be misled by the data on population or total harvest for the species you plan to hunt. The important criterion is the hunter success rate, which is always figured on a percentage basis. For example, if a state had a general success rate of 23 percent for deer, that means 23 out of 100 hunters took a deer.

This figure doesn't always tell the truth, because states often lump all hunts together. Nor does it indicate the success rate for specific areas or for restricted, or "quality," hunts. You need to dig for that information. Take California, for example. This state has one of the highest deer populations in the West, but offers the poorest hunter success rate, consistently less than 10 percent. However, there are units in the state that offer outstanding hunting opportunities, with hunter success rates at 50 percent and higher. Those units require a lottery draw; there is plenty of competition for tags. If you can draw a tag in one of those units, you can enjoy hunting as good as that in the popular Rocky Mountain deer states.

In some states hunter success figures are public information, but in others you must ask. That's where your research should start.

Don't write for information. You'll get many more details over the phone. Initial sources of information are state wildlife agencies. Start by calling the headquarters office (telephone numbers listed state-by-state in Part III) to find out the telephone number of the regional office you're interested in. (States are divided into regions, with a central office in each.) Ask to talk to a big game biologist, game warden, environmental specialist, or whoever is available. Foresters and wildlife biologists with federal land management agencies, particularly the U.S. Forest Service and Bureau of Land Management, can be very helpful as well.

Be as inquisitive as you can, and don't be timid. If you're stymied by an officious-sounding receptionist who won't allow you to speak to an employee, ask if hunting success figures are public information. If so, tell him or her what you're interested in, and request the best means of obtaining the information you want.

Some individuals who work for government agencies aren't fond of answering hunter's questions, but most will open up to you if you're polite and not overly aggressive. I worked as a forester and wildlife biologist for state and federal agencies for sixteen years, and welcomed the opportunity to chat with hunters who requested information. It was a refreshing break from a routine that often involved boring desk projects, and I enjoyed talking with hunters who were astute enough to seek information for a do-it-yourself hunt.

Here are some specific questions to ask when researching hunting areas.

"What is the hunter success rate?" Areas with a rate of 25 percent or less should be looked upon with skepticism. One out of four isn't good; try for units that have 40 percent or better. If you're hunting a western state, find out if the percentages are skewed by outfitters in the area. Many outfitters have very high success hunts, while hunters on their own have very low success hunts. The reason is the outfitter's ability to pack into remote regions and his knowledge of game country.

The fact that you're a nonresident doesn't necessarily mean you'll have poor success, however. It's a fact that nonresident hunters have far higher success rates than residents when the two are compared on non-outfitted hunts. The reason is nonresidents simply try harder, hunt longer, and invest more money in a hunt. Residents often hunt on weekends or make one-day forays.

"What kind of access do the units have?" The answer to this question will determine your ability to travel in the unit, and will provide insight to competition from other hunters. Areas riddled by roads will no doubt have plenty of hunter pressure. This information will also help you determine the kind of vehicle you'll need. Some hunting units may be accessible only by way of four-wheel drive vehicles.

"What are the opportunities for taking a trophy-class animal?" If a big rack interests you, this is the first question you should ask. Wildlife officers can often give accurate statistics, especially if game-check stations have been active in the areas for a number of years. Many states keep records of trophy-class animals and the units where they're taken. Some states have their own version of trophy-class rankings based on Boone and Crockett measurement procedures.

So far these questions are general. If the wildlife officer you're speaking with is cordial and doesn't mind volunteering information, try these specific questions:

"Where would YOU hunt for a good chance at a legal animal?"

"Where would YOU hunt for a good chance at a trophy-class animal?"

In both cases, make it clear that you aren't interested in learning the wildlife officer's personal hotspots. He or she isn't going to tell you anyway. The two key words in the questions are *good chance*. They give your contact some leeway, and you won't sound pushy. If you asked, "Where do YOU hunt?", you'd be treading on hallowed ground.

"How much public land is available?" You'll need to know how much land you can actually hunt on. If you're planning to hunt a national

forest, you'll have plenty of acreage to roam. But you're not assured of a place to hunt just because there are blocks of national forest or Bureau of Land Management lands interspersed with private lands. In many cases, early homesteaders settled in the fertile valley bottoms and ignored the peripheral mountains. Today, those private lands will likely be fenced and posted, and though the best hunting may be on public land in the surrounding mountains, access may be effectively blocked because of locked private gates in the valleys. This is a major problem in much of the West.

"Do any private landowners allow access, either free or for a trespass fee?" Much of the best hunting is on private land for obvious reasons. Hunting is restricted, and game is less disturbed than on public land. These days it's tough to find private landowners who will allow you to hunt for free, particularly if you're a nonresident.

Expensive leases are the rule instead of the exception in many states, and leasing has caught on big in the West. In Colorado, for example, you'd be hard pressed to find a rancher who will allow you to hunt at no charge; the best areas are leased long in advance of hunting season by groups of hunters or outfitters. Nonetheless, there are ranchers who will let you on for free or a modest trespass fee. You'll have to look hard to find them.

You're more apt to find free or inexpensive hunting on private lands where big game animals damage crops. In Wyoming, antelope and deer wreak havoc where they're plentiful, and ranchers often welcome hunters. Wyoming landowners have an added incentive to allow hunting. Attached to every hunting license is a landowner coupon. When you kill an animal, you give the coupon to the landowner whose property you hunted. He turns the coupon in to a game warden and is paid $8 for each animal harvested. The system has its advantages: The rancher is happy because he is reimbursed for some of the crop damage caused by big game animals, and he in turn is apt to allow hunting on his property. The hunter is happy because of increased hunting opportunities.

The best way to find out about hunting private land is the old-fashioned way. Walk up to the door and knock. If the landowner says no, ask if there are other farmers or ranchers in the area that might allow hunting. Obviously this is one method of locating new hunting areas that you can't do by phone or by mail, unless you have some advance information. It's always best to ask permission in person if you're dealing with strangers. Of course, your telephone research will enable you to get as much information as possible before you make your visit.

Once you've settled on an area, be sure to apply early for a license if there's a deadline or quota. In most states, you can buy a big game license prior to or during the season, but in the West the best states require a lottery draw or operate on a first-come–first-serve system for nonresidents. In Wyoming, for example, nonresident elk and deer applications must be in by February 1 and March 15 respectively. In Idaho and Montana, there is a quota on nonresident deer and elk tags; they're sold on a first-come basis. You'll receive no sympathy from a state agency if your application is late. It will be firmly rejected, so pay attention to application instructions.

If you've done your homework right, and if you've drawn a permit (if a lottery was required), your next job is to find all out you can about the country you intend to hunt.

Again, the phone will be your best research tool. Be sure to have a pencil and pad handy to record the information you obtain. The purpose of your initial telephone conversations was to locate general hunting areas. Now you need to focus in on ridges, valleys, drainages, and precise spots within the hunting unit. Use the same sources that you used before to ferret out as much information as possible.

A basic requirement is to get the most detailed, most up-to-date maps you can find. The U.S. Forest Service has maps for each of their national forests across the country, and the Bureau of Land Management has state and district maps. Write to each agency and ask for the maps they have available. Some maps are free, others cost $2 or less. Aside from public land maps that show major drainages, land boundaries, and roads, you should order topographic maps published by the U.S. Geological Survey. Their maps show details the others don't, including contours, tiny drainages, pack and old jeep trails, marshes, and other features that could help you plan your hunt. For maps east of the Mississippi, write the U.S. Geological Survey, 536 National Center, Reston, VA 22092; for maps west of the Mississippi, write the U.S. Geological Survey, Box 25046, Federal Center, Denver, CO 80225.

Study the maps, and with the information you've obtained by talking to agency employees, circle the areas they mentioned. Jot down the names of roads in the map margin, and any other references. When you're done, you should have a map with several options drawn on it, and some sort of strategy in mind.

If possible, *do* scout the area before hunting season. This is common advice, but few hunters follow it. Remember, up to now you have information from phone conversations and a few maps. The next and final step before hunting is to physically look over the land and make some basic decisions about where you'll hunt.

Before you scout, make it a point to stop at the wildlife or forest agency office to get as much updated information as possible. Ask about

Jim Zumbo, left, shakes hands with a pal after a successful Colorado elk hunt. They took their elk on public land in an area crowded with hunters. They did it by scouting in advance of the season and locating elk first.

the condition of the roads, places to camp, and once again ask about areas to hunt in. When you drive to the unit, talk to ranchers, farmers, forest workers, loggers, surveyors, sheepherders, and anyone else who might be able to give you first-hand information.

If you have time, corroborate the information you've received with locals. Go to a sporting goods store and chat with clerks. Get a haircut and talk to the barber. Have a beer or a soft drink in a local tavern and talk with the patrons and bartender. This might seem to be an exercise in futility; as an outsider you may feel like the locals are putting you on. That's the case now and then, but generally folks are sincere and try to help. A last-minute inquiry might prove to be the best move you made.

You can't do too much planning for a hunt. The more the better, and the result of your work could very well be a handsome animal that you'll always cherish.

Application Tips

As soon as you've decided to hunt in the West, write to each state you're interested in for big game hunting information. If it isn't available for the current season, the state will put your name on a mailing list and send it to you as soon as it's printed. Ask for last year's information to get an idea of the system.

Many states publish big game data in a pamphlet or newspaper type tabloid. Because of the variety of species and special hunts, the literature can be complicated, if not downright confusing. Read the application thoroughly – a simple mistake on the form can nullify your application and ruin your hunting plan. Double-check the codes and be certain all questions are answered.

It's wise to send a cashier's check, or postal or bank money order instead of a personal check. Some states will not accept personal checks, or if they do, the check is first cleared before your application data is transferred to a computer. A mistake in your checking account balance could void your application.

Don't wait until a few days before deadline to mail your application. Do it well in advance. If you must wait until the last minute, check to see if the deadline refers to the postmark of the application envelope or the day the application reaches the proper license office.

Some states have preference points for limited entry licenses. This means if you fail to draw a license, you receive points and your application goes into a pile with better odds the following year, and so on. This information will be indicated in the big game literature.

If the state you're applying for requires you to select a region or unit instead of a general statewide license, be judicious when you determine the area. Try to get as much information as possible. Find out how many licenses are available, and ask the state wildlife agency about past odds as well as number of applicants per unit. Some states have this data readily available while others do not.

Gearing up for Your Western Hunt

Since western hunting can involve a long hunt in a remote area, or at least a hunt in the mountains where weather can cause problems, you must be properly equipped before you leave your home. Here's a checklist of gear you should bring, including the essentials as well as a few luxury items that take little space and will make your hunt much more enjoyable. Assume that consideration of space and weight will limit your cargo – that's almost always the case, especially if you're with an outfitter, heading into the backcountry with horses.

Camp Gear If you're hunting on your own, you'll need plenty of equipment. A warm shelter is the primary consideration. Camp vehicles such as trailers, cab-over campers, and motor homes solve the comfort problem, but if you must use a tent you'll have to bring extra equipment.

Make sure the tent is waterproof, even if the manufacturer claims it to be so. If it's supposed to be, don't believe it. If you read the instructions that come with the tent, you'll see where each seam – even on the superior Goretex tents – must be sealed. Many tents will have a tube of sealant in the package it was packed in. If not, buy a tube. Before the hunt, set the tent up in your backyard and seal it thoroughly. Every stitch must be treated.

Cots are a good idea because they keep you off the ground and are comfortable. They take up space, but they're worth it. Bring cots if you're hunting on your own; outfitters will provide them.

A heater is often an essential. A collapsible wood stove will suffice, and it doubles as a cooking stove. A catalytic heater works well, but I've yet to see one keep a tent warm during very cold weather, especially if the wind is blowing. A kerosene heater will work and will take off the chill. A regular camp stove that runs on white gas or propane is adequate for cooking. Have a plentiful supply of fuel on hand. Whatever you use, be sure your sleeping area is well ventilated.

A light source inside the tent is necessary. Most hunters use a single- or double-mantle lantern. They run on white gas or propane. The propane type is self-contained with a disposable can, but the white gas model is traditional and gives you a few seconds to jump into the sleeping bag when you turn it off at night. The propane type goes out immediately when you turn the knob.

Firewood is often an important consideration around camp. Bring a sharp axe as well as a file to keep it sharp. You'll no doubt bring along a favorite camp knife, as well as one to carry in your pocket.

As far as equipment to cut up your game with, bring appropriate tools. If your're hunting elk, take a good saw, boning knife, and hatchet. A small block and tackle will help hoist meat off the ground. Meat sacks and fifty feet of rope round out the list.

Sleeping Gear If you're hunting with an outfitter, you'll be expected to provide your own sleeping bag, unless you're staying in a lodge with beds and linens. In that case, you will be so advised. But most western hunters will spend the night in a sleeping bag.

Down bags are wonderful, though they can be a major problem if you're tent camping and don't have a stove to dry wet items. Down is warm when it's dry, but cold and clammy when it's wet. It's far better to sleep in a bag filled with synthetic fibers, such as Quallofill, Hollofill, or Fiberfill. They are comfortable when damp, and they dry quickly.

Bring a bag rated for very cold temperatures, whether or not you'll be sleeping in a heated tent. Be assured the fire in the stove will go out a couple hours after you retire, and the air temperature inside the tent will quickly match that of the air outside. I know plenty of hunters who brought summer bags on a hunt, and spent many miserable nights because of it.

Put your sleeping bag in a heavy-duty plastic trash bag, and then put it in another one just for good measure. The trash bag will keep it dry while it's being transported into camp. Sleeping bags have a way of getting damp if the weather is moist, no matter how carefully they're packed.

If you expect to sleep on a cot, which is normally the case in tent camps, ask the outfitter if he provides foam pads for the cots. If not, bring your own. It will make all the difference in the world for sleeping comfort. Besides providing the extra cushion, the cot will provide insulation beneath you. Though you might have a warm sleeping bag rated at minus-zero temperatures, there's no loft underneath because your weight compresses the bag. As a result, the cold air in the tent will make you most uncomfortable.

Bring a small pillow. It's a nice luxury that takes little space and you'll appreciate it after a tough day hunting.

Clothing Prepare for every possible kind of weather, because you'll get it in the West. If you're hunting early, and the weather is balmy, wear whatever trousers are comfortable and several light shirts. I usually wear a couple of flannel shirts over an undershirt. If the weather turns extremely warm, I shuck a shirt and stuff it in my daypack – which I *always* carry. I store a heavy woolen jacket in my daypack along with gloves in the event a cold front moves in. For footwear, I wear a pair of cotton woolen socks, and a pair of lightweight, waterproof hiking boots.

If the weather turns cold, I wear polypropylene longjohns, warm trousers, two wool shirts, a down vest, and a woolen jacket over my upper torso. I usually wear two pairs of woolen socks and insulated, waterproof boots. For my hands I wear a pair of lightweight cotton gloves topped by a pair of leather gloves. A warm hat protects my head, and a bandanna around my throat keeps my neck warm.

For late hunting in snow and rain, I wear lots of wool. First, the polypropylene longjohns, then wool pants, wool shirts, and wool jacket. Two pairs of wool socks encased in a pair of pacs with felt liners and leather uppers and rubber bottoms keep my feet warm as toast. A Goretex slicker or overcoat is a must to keep me dry, and gloves and hat keep the rest of me warm. I like plenty of wool in wet weather because wool wicks when it's damp and actually retains heat and keeps you warm. Wool is more expensive than most other garments, but it's worth its weight in gold when you're out hunting and the weather is wet and miserable.

A pair of moccasins or casual shoes to lounge around in camp are nice. If your clothes get wet while you're hunting, you can usually dry them quickly near the woodstove. Dirt is another matter. Don't strive for extreme cleanliness in camp by bringing a dozen shirts and trousers. You can keep your body clean with plenty of soap and warm water, but don't fuss about your looks. No one will care how you look, because you'll all look rather unkept and untidy by the time the hunt nears its end.

If you're worried about blisters or sores on your feet, bring a supply of moleskin. It might very well save the hunt if your feet give you problems.

A note about hunter orange apparel. Most western states require orange for safety reasons. Don't buy a cheap 99-cent plastic vest. It will shred and tear the first time you walk or ride through vegetation. Buy a good article of clothing and avoid nylon because it's noisy in the brush. The same goes for raingear. Buy sturdy apparel that will last.

A final word of advice. If you're riding into camp on horseback with an outfitter, tie a warm jacket and raingear behind your saddle with straps. I've seen more than one hunter start a trip with light clothing on a balmy morning, and I've seen outfitters cuss and moan when the hunter got cold on the way in and asked the outfitter to unpack a horse and find a jacket.

Personal Gear   Bring whatever items you normally use in your bathroom at home. Store your articles in a sturdy toilet kit that is big enough to accommodate your needs. You might also want to bring along extra items, such as a laxative, diarrhea preventative, antacid medication, effervescent tablets, aspirin, cough syrup, antibiotics, and any other medication you might need. If you take prescribed medication regularly, be certain you have an adequate supply.

By all means, have a dependable flashlight. Of late, I've been hauling around two or three of the disposable type. They're small, lightweight, and easy to use and store.

A first-aid kit is handy for minor cuts and bruises. The outfitter will have one, but I like to carry my own as well.

If you enjoy a libation before or after dinner, bring your own. Outfitters normally don't provide liquor. One bottle of your favorite should suffice. Don't overdo it and expect the outfitter to pack in a case of wine or beer for you. Liquids are heavy, and weight should be kept to a minimum. If you're camping on your own and weight is no problem, bring whatever strikes your fancy.

Daypack I bring along a daypack wherever I hunt. It holds a small first aid kit, and a survival kit that includes waterproof matches, mirror, candle, fishhooks, fishing line, reliable flashlight, space blanket, fifty feet of rope, small block and tackle, collapsible meat saw, sharpening stone, extra cartridges, wool jacket, film, a bag of hard candy, and trail food that I make up myself (assorted goodies such as sunflower seeds, raisins, coconut, almonds, peanuts). On top of all this I place my camera so it's handy.

Many outfitters will provide their own checklist of equipment. Follow their instructions carefully. When packing gear, use soft duffle bags, never hard suitcases. Bring a soft case for your gun. Chances are you'll put your gun in the scabbard when you leave the trailhead if you're riding a horse, and I guarantee no outfitter will pack a hard gun case into camp unless you know something I don't. You should use the hard case to transport the gun from home to the West, and then store it while you're hunting.

If you're unsure of the gear needed for your particular hunt, consult a friend who is an experienced hunter or ask your outfitter or booking agent. When in doubt, the key is warm and dry. An uncomfortable hunter is a poor hunter. Make it easy on yourself and be prepared, but don't overdo it with unnecessary gear.

Getting West and Transporting Your Game Home

Proper handling of your big game from the place of kill to the butchering site, and then home, is a crucial aspect of a successful hunt. Meat must be carefully tended to in order to get it packaged for storage in quality condition.

The planning begins even before you pull the trigger. The key word is *cold*. It's imperative to cool the flesh immediately after the animal is dead. Just a few hours' delay can result in spoiled meat.

Field-dressing, the first step in caring for game, must be done as soon as possible. A big game animal must be gutted as soon as it's down.

When a deer is killed, the decision to skin it immediately after field-dressing depends on the air temperature and other circumstances. If you must leave the carcass overnight and drag it out the next day, it's best to leave it unskinned and hang it in the shade of a tree. The skin will protect the meat when the animal is being dragged. If the carcass is in camp or you can get close to it in a vehicle, skin it right away if the weather is warm. I seldom skin my deer until I get it home or to camp, though I've made exceptions in hot weather.

I do most of my hunting at high elevations where fall temperatures are relatively low, but there are plenty of big game seasons around the West when the temperature can hit 90 degrees with evening lows of 60 or 70 degrees. Bowhunting seasons usually run in early fall when the days are balmy. Antelope seasons are often in September; I've hunted pronghorns when daytime temperatures hovered around 100 degrees. Again, think *cold* once the animal is down.

If you're hunting antelope, skin the carcass quickly, no matter what the temperature. Antelope fur is dense and retains body heat remarkably well. Most experienced pronghorn hunters I know skin their animals within an hour after the kill.

Elk must also be skinned immediately, particularly the heavily furred neck. I killed a big bull in Idaho recently, and by the time my pal and I dressed it, darkness was almost upon us. We had a long climb up a mountain to our horses and a seven-mile ride to base camp. We skinned part of the front quarters but didn't complete skinning the neck. The air temperature was getting down to about 25 degrees at night and we planned to return early the following morning with pack horses. The next morning, I was amazed to find that the neck was still very warm. Some of the meat already had a suspicious odor, but we trimmed away a small portion and managed to salvage most of it. Another few hours, however, and I'm sure the neck would have been ruined.

Cooling the meat of your quarry is only one aspect of getting it from the West to your table. Transporting it to your home or storage locker is the next, particularly if home is more than a thousand miles away. Four modes of travel are possible: a motor vehicle, an airplane, a train, or a bus. The first two are the most popular.

Riding a bus is the poorest way for a hunter to travel because of one very important reason: Greyhound and Continental Trailways, our two major bus carriers, do not allow firearms to be transported in the baggage compartment. On the other hand, a bus can be satisfactory for shipping meat, but there are restrictions. Meat can be shipped only if it's frozen and packed with dry ice. Greyhound's policy requires the meat to reach its destination within 24 hours; Continental Trailways has an 18-hour time limit. Although the time factor precludes shipping meat from the Rocky Mountain region to East Coast cities, destinations in the South and on the West Coast could be within reach.

The cost of shipping meat depends on the weight of the package and the distance the package is to be shipped. For specific rate information,

Getting an elk out is a real challenge. Look at the size of this animal. It will weigh 800 to 1,000 pounds on the hoof. Think hard about how you'll get an animal out if you kill one far from a road and have no horses.

call your local bus terminal or the headquarters office. For baggage information, call Greyhound headquarters in Phoenix, (602) 248–4058, or Continental Trailways headquarters in Dallas, (214) 655–7960.

Firearms are allowed aboard some Amtrak railway systems if they are shipped as checked baggage. Rifles must be broken down and firing mechanisms removed. Ammunition is not allowed. Foodstuffs cannot be checked as passenger baggage, although they can be sent as separate freight. Meat must be frozen, packed in dry ice, and shipped at the owner's risk. For information on current rates, contact Amtrak, (800) USA–RAIL.

There are two disadvantages to using any rail system: delivery is slow, meaning meat might spoil before arriving at its destination, and rail centers are not always in convenient locations as far as hunters are concerned.

The U.S. Post Office will ship frozen meat without restrictions. Dry ice can be used as long as the package is leakproof. Express mail, which guarantees one- to two-day delivery (depending on the area) is the best way to send frozen meats. Up to 70 pounds per package is allowed.

The United Parcel Service will ship meat packed with dry ice by ground transportation only. UPS considers dry ice as a hazardous substance (since it gives off carbon dioxide, which displaces oxygen) and will not allow it to be shipped as air cargo. However, UPS will ship frozen meat without dry ice by air, but is not responsible if the meat spoils. The maximum weight allowed by the company is 70 pounds. Delivery time is five working days, which is a poor option for shipping chilled or frozen meat. UPS also offers "Next Day Air" and "Second Day Air"; rates for both are standard regardless of shipping points.

Federal Express will ship meat packed with dry ice in one to two business days. If five pounds or less of dry ice is used, the package will not be considered a restricted item and will be transported according to standard procedures. More than five pounds of dry ice requires additional fees and restrictions.

Whether you ship meat by bus, rail, the Post Office, UPS, or one of the "quick delivery" services, check in advance before you show up with your meat at the agent's counter. Rates vary widely according to the weight of your package, destination, and type of service you desire. You might also be dealing with an agent who isn't aware of company policies and procedures, especially in locations that don't carry a large volume of hunter business.

If you choose to drive a vehicle and intend to bring large amounts of meat home, a rental trailer is an affordable option. Rates are based on the size of the trailer and mileage incurred while towing. The four-by-six-foot trailer is the smallest available, and I calculated it would easily accommodate meat from four elk, four mule deer, four antelope, and more. (The trailers are covered and stand five feet high.)

If you fly, the cheapest and easiest way to transport meat is to check it free as baggage. In order to do so, though, you must have baggage that does not exceed the limits set by airlines. For example, Western Airlines allows two pieces of baggage to be checked and one to be hand-carried. Both pieces to be checked must not exceed 140 pounds. If you're checking one suitcase, you can check a package of meat as long as the two do not exceed 140 pounds.

From a practical standpoint, however, you'll be hard pressed to go on a hunting trip with only one suitcase or dufflebag. You'll need at least two pieces, which means you'll have to pay excess baggage to ship an additional piece. But rates are reasonable, making air transport an economical and safe way to ship game meat home.

If you aren't flying, you can still ship your meat via an airline. Just make sure you're aware of any restrictions concerning the use of dry ice.

How do you pack meat for transportation? The procedure depends on the condition of the meat and the duration of the trip. If you're hunting in the Rockies and will fly home, it's usually possible to freeze the meat, wrap it securely, and check it as baggage without dry ice. To do this, allow the meat to remain in a freezer until the last possible moment, and get it to your freezer or storage locker as soon as you arrive at your destination.

Some time ago, I transported 40 pounds of frozen, packaged elk meat from Denver to New York. I wrapped each package in five or six sheets of newspaper, packed them in three heavy-duty trash bags, and sealed each with a twist-tie. I stuffed wadded newspaper in the bottom of a cardboard carton, inserted the bag of elk meat, and jammed more wadded paper into every nook and cranny. When I arrived, the meat was still hard frozen with no sign of thawing, although it had been out of the freezer for almost 10 hours.

A friend who hunts deer in Texas every season annually returns with three deer for the freezer. He bones the meat carefully, freezes it, and ships it home as excess baggage in two extra-large duffle bags.

By boning an animal before you ship it, you save a great deal of space and weight. An average, mature deer will yield 75 to 125 pounds of boned, trimmed meat; an average antelope will weigh about 35 to 40 pounds when boned; and an elk will tip the scales at 200 to 350 pounds when boned.

If you don't know how to bone meat, you can have it done professionally, but you'll need to allow an extra day or two from the time you leave hunting camp to the time you leave for home. During hunting season, meat plants are at their busiest, and you may have to wait a few days before your meat is processed. If you're hunting with an outfitter, ask him or a guide to bone the meat for an extra fee.

If all else fails, you can bone the meat yourself. It's easy to do. I use a long, flexible-blade knife and simply cut big chunks away from the bone. A fish fillet knife (available in any sporting goods store) also works well.

If you ship boned meat, it's best not to freeze it since it will then have to be thawed, butchered into small cuts, and refrozen. Just chill the meat if you intend to put it on an airplane and can get it to a cooler or refrigerator within six to eight hours.

To freeze meat for shipment, it should be completely cut and wrapped to your specifications. With that done, you can simply toss it in the freezer when you get home. You can have the meat cut and wrapped by a butcher before you leave for home, or you can do it yourself. I can cut and wrap an antelope in two hours and a deer in four. An elk takes much more time, and bigger tools are required.

If you drive your own vehicle, there are several ways to get your game home. Skin the animal, quarter it, and chill the meat thoroughly, then tightly wrap the quarters in a heavy quilt, an old sleeping bag, or several layers of blankets. As you drive, keep the meat out of the sunlight. If you stop at a motel in the evening and the night air is cold, unwrap the meat and allow the air to circulate around it.

If you box the meat and transport it frozen or chilled, you can use a cardboard carton, cooler, or homemade container. Inexpensive Styrofoam coolers are ideal for shipping as are regular coolers used for camping. You can buy corrugated cardboard boxes from meat packers or locker plants. Many hunters prefer to use a specially insulated homemade box.

Dry ice is best to keep meat cold or frozen when traveling. About 10 pounds of dry ice is sufficient to keep 40 to 80 pounds of frozen meat intact for 24 hours. Dry ice should be placed on top of the meat, and the container sealed tightly. If the meat is not frozen, 20 pounds of dry ice for the same weight and time period should suffice. Some dry ice should be placed in the middle of the meat packages and the rest on top. The meat will probably freeze where it's resting against the dry ice.

Another option in transporting meat is to trade venison for readymade sausage and salami. Most large towns have locker plants that perform this service. You simply bring your animal to a meat plant and trade it for an equal amount of assorted sausages and the like. If you have 35 pounds of boned antelope, you'll receive 35 pounds of preprocessed meat. State laws don't allow you to buy wild game, but you can often trade it and buy salami and sausage made from elk, deer, and antelope. Since the packer adds beef suet to the meat, you're entitled to buy an additional 10 or 20 percent.

Prices vary according to the four or five kinds of meat often sold: Polish sausage, summer sausage, breakfast sausage, kielbasa, and salami. Ask to try samples of the different meats before you trade. You probably won't be getting the meat from *your* animal in the trade because it all goes into a huge pot and is processed equally. I've never been dissatisfied with the products I've purchased, and I've dealt with six different packing houses in the Rockies.

The question of aging game meat always comes up when preparing it for transportation. While it's true that aging an animal for four or five days prior to butchering it improves the texture, you may not have the time to do so. It's better to cut up and package the animal and deal with it later if you have no other choice. Venison can be marinated or cooked slowly in a crockpot or casserole dish it it's a bit tough.

Make it a priority to ship your meat home from the West in quality condition. You won't be sorry when you sit down at the dinner table.

II

A Look At Western Big Game Animals

Now let's take a good look at the big-game animals in the West. Besides providing general information about each species, I've included specifics on the following:

Hunting Tactics Tips and techniques commonly used.

Best States Where to find optimal hunting.

Firearms Best rifles for each species, along with reasons why some rifles are superior to others.

Trophies There are three listings: the first represents the totals in the latest Boone and Crockett book (8th Edition); the second shows the heads taken from 1975 to 1980 as listed in the 8th edition; and the third provides data from the interim edition, which classifies trophies accepted from 1980 to 1982.

A word about deer: There are three major deer species in the West: the Rocky Mountain muley, the blacktail, and the whitetail. The Coues deer, a diminutive whitetail, lives in southern Arizona and New Mexico.

The blacktail and Rocky Mountain mule deer are close cousins, and differ basically in their environments and the size of their antlers. There are also several other mule deer subspecies in the West. To simplify the western deer, I'll focus on the three major species mentioned above.

Antelope

Of all the big game species to hunt in the West, antelope are by far the easiest. Hunter success ranges 90 percent and better in many states.

Antelope are comparatively easy quarry because they're highly visible and often very plentiful. Depending on their eyesight for security, they shun brushy and forested areas. In some areas, it's not unusual to see several hundred antelope in a day, and on public land where access is good.

Most of the public land inhabited by antelope is administered by the U.S. Bureau of Land Management. Maps are available from BLM state and district offices, but be sure you have updated, clear maps. In many western states, landowners do not post their land; it's up to you to know where you are.

In ranch and farm areas, antelope often cause crop damage. Landowners are apt to permit free hunting or charge a modest trespass fee. In areas where trophy antelope are taken, you might have to pay a higher fee if the landowner hasn't already leased the area to an outfitter or group of hunters.

Because antelope live in the lowlands throughout most of their range, plenty of roads cross their domain. Many roads are paved or graveled, allowing access to cars and two-wheel drive vehicles. Other areas might require four-wheel drives. While planning your hunt, be sure to inquire as to the condition of the roads.

Most antelope hunts occur in September and early October, but don't be fooled by the weather. A day or two of rain will turn most desert roads into soup, and you'll be hard pressed to move, even with chains and a four-wheel drive. All you can do is wait for the roads to dry.

Since antelope dwell in low elevations and are accessible, they offer a fine opportunity for a low-cost, do-it-yourself hunt. In many places you can forego camping equipment and base out of a motel. My own choice is to tent camp in a hidden ravine surrounded by sagebrush, where there is no sound of traffic and I can hear coyotes in the night.

Be prepared for warm weather as well as storms. Carry a large cooler, and be ready to skin, quarter and chill an antelope as soon as it's dispatched.

Hunting Tactics   The standard method is to spot antelope herds in the distance from a vehicle, glass them over with a spotting scope or binoculars, and then make a stalk on foot if a good buck is located. You'll need to use all your stalking skills, because an antelope's eyesight is superb. Unless you can take advantage of low vegetation, hills, gullies, rocky outcrops and draws, you won't get very close.

Another technique is to make a drive on foot with companions, but keep in mind that antelope aren't directed very well from one place to another. If fences are available, you can usually count on animals running along them until they find a place to go under. Antelope seldom jump fences.

An ambush near a waterhole works fine, but you'll need to be out of sight and stay quiet. This tactic is best for hunters who must get close, such as bowhunters and muzzleloader hunters. Antelope may water anytime during the day. Patience is a must.

Unfortunately, some hunters dismiss antelope as less than worthy quarry and chase them with vehicles. This is illegal, immoral, and unethical, but a minority of hunters do it.

Best States Without a doubt, Wyoming is the top state for antelope. Over the last several years, more than 100,000 tags have been offered annually. This amounts to more antelope harvested than there are live antelope in the rest of the western states combined. Although Wyoming requires a lottery draw with a traditional March 15 application deadline, thousands of tags are left over after the drawing and are sold on a first-come basis. Plenty of tags are unsold each year. Colorado and Montana have good antelope hunting, with tags offered in a lottery. Chances of drawing tags vary each year, depending on the severity of the previous winterkill and the size of the herds. Arizona and New Mexico have good antelope hunting, with some of the biggest bucks taken from private ranches, though public lands yield big bucks as well. Other western states offer antelope hunting, with the bulk of the tags allotted to residents. Only Washington has no antelope season.

Firearms Since long shots are often the rule in antelope country, a flat-shooting rifle is recommended. Favorites include the .243, .25/06, .270, and .30/06. Most hunters sight their rifles at 150 or 200 yards. A scope is helpful for long distance shots. I suspect ninety-five percent of all antelope hunters use a riflescope.

Trophies Wyoming leads the list, but you won't find trophies everywhere in the state. Focus your efforts in and around Carbon County in the south. Most trophies come from this region. For the best odds of taking a trophy, Arizona and New Mexico have more record animals in their herds proportionately. California and Oregon also have big bucks, but only residents can hunt. Recently, Nevada has been issuing a few tags to nonresidents. Some very good bucks inhabit Nevada, and your chances for a B&C buck here are excellent. According to the Boone and Crockett book, 451 antelope are listed. Here's where they came from.

Wyoming	202	South Dakota	9
Arizona	62	North Dakota	7
Montana	34	Nebraska	6
New Mexico	29	Idaho	4
Oregon	21	Saskatchewan	3
Nevada	16	Mexico	2
Colorado	15	Kansas	1
Alberta	13	Oklahoma	1
Texas	13	Utah	1
California	12		

1975-1980:

Wyoming	38	Nebraska	3
Arizona	11	Texas	3
New Mexico	11	Alberta	2
California	8	South Dakota	2
Oregon	7	Kansas	1
Montana	6	North Dakota	1
Nevada	5	Saskatchewan	1
Colorado	4	Utah	1

1980-1982:

Wyoming	54	Colorado	4
Nevada	9	California	3
New Mexico	8	Idaho	3
Oregon	8	Texas	3
Montana	7	South Dakota	2
Arizona	6	Utah	1

Bighorn Sheep

Rocky Mountain and desert bighorn sheep live in the lower 48. Competition for tags, especially for desert bighorns, is intense. Just a few states have tags. Montana has a half-dozen hunting units that offer over-the-counter permits for Rocky Mountain bighorns, but hunting stops when a quota is reached. Hunter success is very low in those units, usually less than 10 percent.

If you draw a tag for bighorns, hiring an outfitter is the best option. You can't afford to waste time looking for sheep, and the cost is well worth the outfitter's efforts and expertise. It's possible to find sheep on your own in some areas, but most regions require careful scouting.

Legal rams are designated by the curl of the horn or by age or B&C score. Many states require hunters to take an orientation course in order to identify legal rams.

Hunting Tactics   If you're hunting desert sheep, much of your hunting will be done from a four-wheel drive truck; horses are used in some areas. Most hunting is done by glassing, and you'll no doubt do a lot of walking in extreme heat. To hunt Rocky Mountain sheep, you'll probably ride horses to upper elevations, then walk a great deal. Climbing rocks and steep slopes is usually standard procedure. As in the case with desert sheep, you'll do a lot of glassing.

Be in good physical condition for either species. You'll be under plenty of stress as you hike and climb.

Best States   Desert bighorns are hunted in Arizona, Nevada, Utah, and Mexico. Arizona has produced the most trophy rams, but Nevada has been giving up many in recent years. Rocky Mountain sheep are hunted in most western states. Montana, Wyoming, Colorado, and Idaho are considered top states.

Firearms   Sheep are not necessarily tough, but a good, flat-shooting rifle with sufficient energy is required. Shots might be very long, and under difficult conditions. Know your rifle well before taking a sheep hunt.

Trophies   Of 319 Rocky Mountain sheep listed in the B&C record book, here is the breakdown.

Alberta 166	Colorado 12
British Columbia 46	Unknown 4
Montana 44	Oregon 2
Wyoming 27	North Dakota 1
Idaho....................16	Canada (unknown) 1

1975–1980:

Alberta 13	British Columbia 1
Montana 8	Colorado 1
Oregon 2	Wyoming...................1

1980–1982:

Montana 16	Wyoming 2
Alberta 11	Idaho 1
British Columbia 5	Oregon 1

Of 279 desert sheep in the record book, here is the listing.

Mexico 156	California 14
Arizona 71	New Mexico 1
Nevada 37	

1975–1980:

Mexico 33	Arizona 10
Nevada 14	California .... 1 (picked up)

1980–1982:

Mexico 23	Arizona 15
Nevada 16	

Black Bear

Though black bears are hunted throughout the United States, the West produces most of the trophy class bruins and has some of the highest concentrations of bears. Black bears are often not black-colored in the West. In some states, the majority of bears are cinnamon and brown colored. These are black bears in every sense of the word, and are not to be confused with the brown or grizzly bear.

Bears primarily dwell in forested regions—the more rugged, the more bears. In some areas, bears prey heavily on elk calves. When the problem is severe, wildlife officials have often liberalized seasons to encourage a heavier bear harvest.

Unlike other regions in the country, the West offers good bear hunting in the spring as well as the fall in most states. Spring seasons often start in April and run to early June. Some states allow bear hunting year-long.

When bears emerge from their winter dens, they've lost much weight. Their pelts are prime, however, and remain that way for several weeks. By late May and early June, the pelt becomes thinner and unsightly as the winter fur falls off.

Depending on how you hunt, a do-it-yourself trip is possible. Bears are often spotted from roads in some areas, but you need to know the best places to watch. Spring bears are active and feed heavily to regain

Jim Zumbo is all smiles with a black bear he took in Montana. Although bears are hunted in every region of the country, the West offers excellent spring and fall hunting. In fact, bear harvests from the West are much higher than other regions. Depending on state laws, bears can be hunted over baits, with hounds, or by glassing and stalking.

lost weight, and can often be spotted foraging. In the fall, most bears are taken by hunters who are after other species such as deer or elk.

Hunting Tactics There are three ways to hunt bears in the spring: baiting, chasing them with hounds, and glassing feeding or traveling bruins in forest openings.

Baiting involves depositing some kind of food and watching it until a bear shows up. Bait can be a dead horse, cow, or pig, meat scraps from a slaughterhouse, or anything else that will attract bears. Bears have a keen sense of smell, and will detect a potential meal a long way off. To hunt a baited area, you must sit motionless in a stand and watch for an approaching bear. The best time of day is the hour before dark in late afternoon, so you might have a long wait. Bears that come to a bait aren't pushovers. You need to be ever watchful and alert, since they'll often slip around noiselessly.

Hunting with hounds is popular in many states. This technique involves driving a vehicle, walking, or riding horseback with a pack of hounds sniffing about as you go. If you cross a fresh bear trail, the hounds will let you know instantly. They're turned free and allowed to chase the bear, and you must follow until the bear is bayed or treed. This can be a rugged experience. You'll be running and climbing through the forest, trying to keep up with the sound of the dogs. Bears often refuse to tree, but will stand their ground and fight the dogs. For that reason alone you'll be running at top speed. Most outfitters take a dim view of bears chewing on their hounds.

Glassing bears with a spotting scope or binoculars is effective in the spring. Bears graze on fresh grass extensively, and often show themselves in meadows and clearcuts where visibility is good. In some areas there are so many bears that you can be assured of seeing several over a one-week period. Look for bears late in the afternoon.

In the fall, most bears are killed incidental to the hunting of other species. Many deer and elk hunters buy bear tags just in case they come across a bruin.

Best States Only Nevada has no bear season; the rest offer good hunting. Oregon, Washington, California, Montana and Idaho are among the best in terms of annual harvest. In parts of Idaho, two bears can be taken. Montana hunters may not use hounds or baits; they must take bears by spotting them in the spring or running into them during fall big-game hunts. In most states, bear tags are unlimited. You simply buy them prior to your hunt.

Firearms Guns for bear hunting are the subject of much debate.

Bruins are tough, tenacious, and dangerous if they're wounded. Magnums are favored by many bear hunters, and for good reason. The 7mmMag is popular, and I've known plenty of hunters who use a 375 H&H Magnum and bigger on black bears. This is one species you don't want to mess with. I consider my .30/06 to be at the edge of the light side, and wouldn't recommend anything lighter. Bears can kill people. Use the heaviest gun you can shoot comfortably.

Trophies There are 134 bears listed in the current B&C book. Here's where they were taken.

Arizona	20	Idaho	2
Colorado	19	Minnesota	2
Wisconsin	17	Oregon	2
California	14	Saskatchewan	2
British Columbia	7	Tennessee	2
Wyoming	7	Virginia	2
Alberta	6	Louisiana	1
Washington	6	Mexico	1
Alaska	5	Michigan	1
Pennsylvania	4	New Mexico	1
Utah	4	Newfoundland	1
Manitoba	3	Nova Scotia	1
New York	3	Ontario	1

1975–1980:

Arizona	7	Colorado	2
British Columbia	3	Wyoming	2
Utah	3	Manitoba	1
Wisconsin	3	Minnesota	1
Alberta	2	Virginia	1
California	2		

1980–1982:

Arizona	4	Alaska	1
Colorado	4	Alberta	1
Saskatchewan	4	California	1
Wisconsin	4	Montana	1
British Columbia	2	New York	1
Pennsylvania	2	Utah	1
Wyoming	2		

Blacktail Deer

This close relative of the muley inhabits the thick rain forests of the West Coast from the Cascade Range to the ocean. For the most part, blacktails are hunted by locals; few nonresidents travel to the West Coast to hunt them, perhaps because they're tough to hunt and don't have the impressive antlers of the larger Rocky Mountain mule deer.

Hunting Tactics   Because they live in dense forests, hunters look for them in clearcuts and forest openings as the deer feed in early morning or late afternoon. Another technique is to slip along quietly, stillhunting in the timber and hoping to see a deer before it sees you. Driving also works, and hunters commonly take them from tree stands by watching trails.

Best States   Blacktail deer are hunted in California, Oregon, and Washington. There are plenty of national forests that provide public hunting, and large timber companies often allow hunting access.

Firearms   Blacktails are smaller than muleys; any big game rifle will suffice. More important than the caliber is the ability to see deer in the timber. Some hunters prefer scopes, others like open sights. If you use a scope, make sure it's waterproof, and use scope caps in extremely rainy weather. Because of the moisture, use a gun with an action that won't jam.

Trophies   California is by far the top state for blacktails. Trinity County and other surrounding counties commonly produce the top racks. The following 309 heads are listed in the Boone & Crockett book.

California 136   Washington. 72
Oregon 89   British Columbia 12

1975–1980:
California 12   Washington. 2
Oregon 2

1980–1982:
California 36   Washington. 10
Oregon 25

Elk

There are two huntable elk subspecies: the Roosevelt's and Rocky Mountain. Roosevelt's, also called Olympic elk, live in the coastal for-

Elk hunting is at its best during the breeding season, and a good guide is invaluable for bugling in a bull, unless you can do it yourself. There are a number of instructional tapes that will teach you how to call before your trip.

ests of the Pacific Northwest. The Rocky Mountain subspecies is a resident of every western state and is hunted in all but California. It is by far the most sought-after animal.

Elk are perhaps the most misunderstood big game animal of all. Many inexperienced hunters believe elk are residents only of remote backcountry regions. Nothing could be further from the truth. Certainly elk do very well in the hinterlands, but they're equally at home in forested areas traversed by roads. Thousands of elk are taken each year by hunters who never venture more than a half mile from their camp or vehicle.

Elk will stay in areas where they aren't disturbed. That doesn't mean a backcountry trek is in order, but that's quite often the only option. However, pockets of brush, small timbered draws, and other isolated spots may be the perfect refuge for elk, even though they're within earshot of paved highways. I've taken two bull elk that bedded in brushy patches adjacent to well-traveled roads.

To the nonresident elk hunter, this means elk hunting need not be an expensive odyssey. Time is the largest outlay in this type of hunting, since it may take several days to locate animals. Unlike deer, elk aren't scattered singly or in small groups throughout the forest. They're generally banded together, and you may have to cover a lot of miles to locate the band.

Be prepared to hunt hard, whether you hunt on your own or with an outfitter. According to Jack Atcheson, Sr., a Montana hunting consultant who has booked thousands of hunts around the world, the elk is the toughest big game animal to hunt in North America. Atcheson, who hunts elk with more zeal and enthusiasm than most people, believes the majority of novice hunters are unaware of the demands of elk hunting.

There's another demand—you've got a big job in front of you when you put an elk to the ground. Getting his carcass out of the forest is no easy task.

You'll find elk basically in the high country, but they live in lowlands, too. In some regions, they're quiet at home in sagebrush areas as well as scrubby juniper forests and oak brush thickets.

The hunter success rate for elk is low, commonly 20 percent or less. To increase your odds, apply for limited-entry areas that require a lottery draw. If you get a tag, you'll have less competition from other hunters with a much better chance of seeing a mature, branch-antlered bull. Bear in mind that spike bulls and small four- or five-point elk are all that exist in many units, especially where hunter pressure is heavy. Think twice about passing up a smallish bull if you have the opportunity. Most elk hunters subscribe to the belief that any elk is a good elk.

Cow and antlerless tags are available in every state as well; consider

After your elk is field-dressed, you'll need to transport the 400 or more pounds of meat out of the woods. Two horses are the best means of transportation. Anything less and you're in for an ordeal.

applying for one of these permits. The best option is an either-sex or hunter's choice tag. If you get one, you have the option of taking any elk.

Hunting Tactics   The bugle season is the finest time to hunt elk. Bulls are breeding and are much more vulnerable during this period, which generally occurs from mid-September to early October. However, most regular elk hunts are held after the bugle period. Apply for early seasons whenever possible. If you can hunt early, learn how to bugle. Buy a call with an instructional tape from a sporting goods store and learn how to use it. Currently, the mouth diaphragm call and grunt tube are state of the art. Learn how to use them and you'll be ready for any bull that walks.

Once serious snows arrive, elk evict the high country and head for winter ranges. Some states have migration hunts, and some have hunts that extend into the snowy season. This is an excellent time to hunt, but be prepared for bad weather. You'll probably find it.

Between the early and late seasons, elk will be sulking in the timber. This is generally the time that most elk seasons open. To hunt these animals, you'll need to pursue them in the forests where they live. Bugle calls won't work, and you'll need to use all your skills to find animals.

Cover plenty of ground quickly, and look for fresh sign. When you find it, slow down and hunt intently. Don't look for a big animal in the timber. Look for a patch of fur, the twitch of an ear, or a bit of sunlight glinting off an antler.

Best States Colorado is the top elk state in terms of elk populations, but you'll find plenty of crowds on public land. The best private ranches are leased, and you'll have trouble finding a place to hunt. Small bulls are prevalent in much of Colorado because of the intense hunting pressure. Bulls just don't have a chance to live long enough to grow big antlers.

Oregon has a similar situation. Montana produces the most trophy elk according to the record book, and Idaho and Wyoming also offer excellent hunting. Arizona and New Mexico have some very big elk, and many people believe a new world record bull will come from Arizona. Alberta also has been producing big bulls lately. A number of private ranches and Indian reservations offer very good hunting in the southwest states.

A big problem nowadays is getting a nonresident elk permit. More and more states are going to a lottery system; you'll have to trust your luck to a computer drawing in the best elk states.

Firearms Elk are big and tough. Though some hunters use light calibers, such as the .243 or .25/06, I'd suggest something more substantial. The 7mmMag is currently a favorite because of its energy and long range capability. I've been using a .30/06 for all my elk hunting, and I'm completely satisfied with it. The most important aspect is using a firearm you can shoot well. An accurate bullet of sufficient energy is the primary consideration.

Trophies In the past, all elk were listed in the record book under the heading, American Elk. Recently, the Boone and Crockett Club separated the Roosevelt's and American elk. It's tough these days to find a B&C bull that must score at least 375. According to the latest B&C Book edition, here's where the records came from. A total of 228 heads are listed.

Montana	61	Unknown	6
Wyoming	42	New Mexico	4
Alberta	29	Saskatchewan	4
Colorado	27	Manitoba	3
Idaho	25	Washington	2
Arizona	18	Texas	1
Oregon	6		

1975–1980:

Montana 6	Idaho 3
Arizona 4	Wyoming 2
Alberta 3	

1980–1982:
American Elk

Montana 4	Oregon 2
Wyoming 4	Alberta 1
Arizona 3	New Mexico 1
Colorado 2	Washington 1

Roosevelt's Elk

Oregon 31	British Columbia 3
Washington 9	California 1

Moose

The Shira's or Wyoming moose inhabits a number of western states. The smallest of the three moose subspecies in North America, it is common in the northern Rockies. Transplant projects have recently established new herds in areas previously uninhabited by moose.

The Wyoming moose is quite at home in timbered stands and generally lives in the upper elevations of mountainous regions. Willow creekbottoms are favored habitats; the moose spend much of their time feeding and bedding in them.

Tags are tough to get, but hunter success is usually very good, often 80 percent or better. The biggest problem in moose hunting is getting them out. In areas where herds are high, antlerless tags are offered.

Hunting Tactics Moose hunters generally scout their area prior to the season and locate individual animals. Moose will often stay in a particular place for an extended period. Once one is located, it's usually easy to find when the season is open. The biggest bulls live in secluded drainages off the beaten track. It takes some work to seek them out. Most hunters use horses to cover as much country as possible.

Moose are active early in the morning, late in the afternoon, and in the night. Look for them early and late. Despite their size, they can bed in a small willow patch and remain hidden in the daytime.

Best States Wyoming is the chief state, with about 8,000 moose living in it. Montana has a good population, and these two states offer essentially the only nonresident tags. Idaho and Utah offer resident hunting;

Moose hunting is excellent in the West, with Wyoming leading the list. Though moose are very big, many can be easily transported from site of kill to a vehicle because they're often found near roads. Using an outfitter is a good idea if you're after moose in the backcountry.

Utah offers a few nonresident tags, and Colorado has a few permits for residents.

Firearms Most hunters like Magnum rifles for moose. They're big animals and can take a lot of punishment. Long shots aren't the rule, but it's always possible to see a good moose some distance away. Scopes aren't necessary in thick willows, but many hunters prefer to use them.

Trophies There are 177 Shira's moose listed in the B&C book. Here is the breakdown.

Wyoming 131	Utah 4
Montana..................25	Washington.................1
Idaho.....................16	

1975–1980:

Wyoming 10	Utah 1
Idaho.....................7	Washington.................1
Montana...................3	

1980–1982:

Wyoming...................8	Utah 4
Montana...................7	Idaho.....................2

Mountain Goat

The mountain goat is more numerous in Canada and Alaska, but there are good populations in several western states. This animal demands very high elevations for its home; it lives on rocky, precipitous slopes that seem impossible for a mammal to negotiate.

States offer either-sex hunting, because it's tough to tell the billies from the nannies. Generally, the male's horns are thicker at the base and have more mass.

Goat seasons often start in September and run into November. Though weather will probably be better in the early part of the season, pelts aren't prime until later.

It's tough to draw a goat tag in most states. If you draw one, an outfitter is a good idea. If you elect to try a hunt on your own, take along one or two pals. It's a bad idea to hunt solo in treacherous areas where goats live.

Hunting Tactics Getting to where the goats live is the toughest part of the hunt. You won't be driving along a road, but you might be able to ride a good share of the way on a horse. For the most part, you'll climb, crawl, and hike. Since goats are white, they can be readily spotted unless they're in the snow. A spotting scope is a great assist. Goats tend to live in certain areas year after year, so you can generally rely on them hanging out in a particular spot. Pay close attention to your footwear. Boots that grip firmly are essential. They could very well be the most important part of your personal gear.

Best States Washington, Montana, and Idaho are tops. Each of these states offers tags to nonresidents. A few tags are available in Wyoming, Colorado, Nevada, and Utah.

Firearms Visibility is often very good in goat country, and long shots are common. A sturdy deer rifle will do, but I'd lean to the heavy side for a very important reason. You want your goat down as soon as possible. A fatally hit or wounded goat that runs off could slide into a spot where you can't get at it.

Trophies There are 338 goats listed in the B&C book. Here's where they came from.

British Columbia	210	Idaho	5
Alaska	70	South Dakota	3
Washington	29	Nevada	2
Montana	11	Yukon	2
Alberta	5	Colorado	1

1975–1980:

British Columbia	22	Idaho	1
Alaska	5	South Dakota	1
Washington	3	Yukon	1
Nevada	2		

1980–1982:

British Columbia	11	Montana	3
Alaska	9	Washington	3

Mountain Lion

Mountain lions, also called cougars in much of the West, are misunderstood by folks who don't live around them. Lions were killed off in most of the East, and a small population is barely holding its own in Florida's Everglades. In the West, however, cougars are alive and well, and are in fact increasing throughout much of their range. Until the 1960s, lions were considered varmints and were bountied year-round. Every western state established regulations protecting lions, and now they're hunted in all the West except California. In most states, quotas are used to determine the annual harvest, and lions are managed in conjunction with mule deer herds. The big cats prey extensively on deer, and are seldom found away from their prey.

Most seasons are held in the winter, generally from December through February or March. Tags are unlimited in most states, though a couple have a lottery draw or a deadline prior to which licenses must be purchased.

Adult lions of either sex are legal in most states, and females with kittens or kittens themselves are protected everywhere.

In top lion areas, you'll be hunting in rimrock and rocky sidehills in and around mule deer winter range. Lions concentrate in these areas, which are at comparatively low elevations.

Hunting Tactics Lion hunting means hounds. That's about the only way to hunt the big cats of the West. Since the canines must be hardy, extremely well-trained dogs, your only choice will be to hire an out-fitter.

The hunt itself will involve a lively chase, its length depending on the freshness of the trail, the terrain, and the energy of the cat. Unlike bears which have plenty of lung power and are apt to be brought to bay on the ground, cougars will almost always tree to escape the dogs. Being typical cats, they don't have the ability to run long and hard; they will likely dash off at high speed for a short distance, then run up a tree. Prepare for a good deal of hiking, though many cougar hunts are relatively short-lived. You can expect to be walking in snow, though this depends on the weather and the area you're hunting. In the Southwest, many hunts are made on dry ground.

Best States Arizona, New Mexico, Colorado, Nevada, Idaho, Montana, and Utah are generally considered the best. Each of these states has a harvest of 150 lions or so annually. There are plenty of outfitters in prime lion country in all the states where lions are plentiful.

Firearms Don't be intimidated by the word *lion*. If the truth were known, I'd suspect more lions have been taken with a .22 or .22 Mag than any other calibers. Consider the fact that your quarry will likely be less than ten yards away, with hounds keeping it motionless in a tree. Not much firepower required, because you can generally pick your target in a vital area. Handguns are standard, though some hunters carry rifles.

Trophies   There are 202 lions listed in the B&C book. Here's where they came from.

British Columbia 39	New Mexico 6
Idaho .28	Wyoming 6
Montana 28	Arizona 5
Utah .22	Nevada 4
Alberta 20	Oregon 4
Washington 20	California 3
Colorado 17	

1975-1980:

British Columbia 11	Colorado 2
Montana 5	Washington 2
Alberta 4	New Mexico 1
Idaho 4	Oregon 1
Utah 4	

1980-1982:

New Mexico 6	Colorado 2
British Columbia 5	Alberta 1
Washington 4	Montana 1
Idaho .3	Utah 1
Oregon 3	

Mule Deer

Prized for its massive antlers, the Rocky Mountain mule deer is the most popular deer in the West, and it accounts for more participation among nonresident hunters than any other big game species. Countless sportsmen make cross-country treks in hopes of seeing a big-racked buck in their rifle sights.

After a general west-wide decline in the mid-1970s, mule deer are recovering nicely in most states. There are so many deer in some regions that antlerless or either-sex permits are available.

Big bucks can be found in all sorts of environments – from greasewood deserts in the low elevations to the rimrock country above timberline. That takes in vast areas of brush, pinyon-juniper forests, quaking aspen stands, and "black" timber or evergreen forests.

A popular way to hunt mule deer is to haul a camp trailer, pick-up camper, or tent into good hunting country and use camp as a central area from which to hunt.

I often use a 19-foot camp trailer pulled behind a four-wheel drive rig if I'm not sure of the country and want to be mobile enough to pull out to a different area.

In places I'm familiar with, I often backpack into good hunting country. The big drawback is the necessity of boning the meat and carrying it out on a packframe. This is a chore not all hunters are equal to because of the obvious physical requirement. I also have horses that I use to help pack out the meat.

Mule deer seasons usually occur in mid-October. Depending on the weather, deer can be in the higher elevations or on their way to lower winter ranges. Mule deer normally migrate from harsh high country areas where winter snow accumulates. It's wise to scout an area before the season, but too much scouting may drive deer out of the area. Restrict your efforts to determining fresh deer use, and look for the quarry during the season.

Some states have early hunts in September when deer are in the high elevations. Big bucks are often in herds, but they'll begin drifting off separately as breeding season nears. The rut normally occurs in November. This is a good time to pursue a mature buck. They follow does to winter range areas and leave the protection of brush and timber. Some states have special post-season hunts in late November and early December, while others have seasons that normally extend into breeding period.

During a recent hunt in Wyoming I was able to hunt several autumn seasons. The first hunt was September 10. I camped at 7,500 feet on the Bridger-Teton National Forest and climbed to 9,000 feet each day, seeking a big buck at or above timberline. I didn't see a deer I wanted, so I returned in mid-October for a crack at a buck during the transition period when they leave the high country and slowly work down to winter range. Still no big buck, so I waited until late November when deer were concentrated in lower elevations, their attention chiefly directed toward breeding. After two days I had the buck I hoped for.

Since I live relatively close by, I was able to be selective and return at will. Most nonresidents don't have this latitude, so it's of paramount importance to pick your season and hunt where the deer are. It would be folly to hunt the lower sagebrush-aspen zones, for example, when the deer are in the higher spruce-fir forests. This altitudinal affiliation is especially prevalent in regions where mountain ranges are about 9,000 to 11,000 feet high.

If you've never hunted mule deer before and want a preview of your quarry, look over several mounted specimens. A cursory tour of two or three western sporting goods stores will no doubt result in plenty of heads to examine.

To the novice hunter used to whitetails, even a small mule deer buck might appear very good if he's running through the timber, or even standing motionless on a sidehill. Use good judgment when you pull the trigger. All your effort and expense may be riding on that one speeding bullet.

A buck with a 30-inch outside spread is considered to be a "standard" trophy-class deer, but this evaluation isn't necessarily true throughout the West. In many areas there are no mule deer of this size. You'll have to look long and hard to see a 30-inch buck. They're hard to find.

Hunting Tactics   Muleys live in differing environments, but a basic strategy is to glass extensively. They feed in open areas early in the morning and late in the afternoon, and you'll need to be looking for them while they're active. Once you spot a deer you want, your next strategy is to stalk close enough for a shot or move in for an ambush, allowing the deer to work close to you.

Another option is to stillhunt, moving slowly and looking for a bedded, walking, or feeding deer. In open country, any brushy spots should be suspect. Muleys like to shade up in heavy cover whenever possible.

My favorite method is to watch for feeding deer at the crack of dawn. As light increases, they start moving to bedding areas. If I haven't found what I'm looking for, I'll head for ridges and walk just below them, stillhunting as I go. I investigate thickets and timbered spots on the way, and invariably manage to find deer.

Don't be afraid to use whitetail tactics on muleys. Many of them work, such as drives and hunting from tree stands. You've probably heard that muleys are stupid in comparison to whitetails. If you believe that and hunt without taking them seriously, you might come up empty on your hunt.

Best States   A number of western states vie for top honors. They include Colorado, Utah, Wyoming, Idaho, and Montana. These are Rocky Mountain states, all of them well-known for good bucks. Arizona and New Mexico have some nice deer, and Nevada is the sleeper. There are good muleys in Nevada, many of them mature bucks, and hunter success is commonly 50 percent or better. Colorado is tops for trophies; they come from scattered areas around the western mountains. There are also prime spots in Idaho and Wyoming where record-class deer can be found. Southeast Idaho is superb, as is the region south of Jackson, Wyoming.

Firearms   It's often said that muleys are much bigger than whitetails

Jim Zumbo packs a mule deer buck and meat on his back. This back-pack holds about 60 pounds of boned meat. Zumbo will make two trips to get all of the deer out. Boning the animal in the woods lightens the load considerably.

and require a powerful gun. That's not true. Whitetails get every bit as big as muleys. Basically, you're dealing with an animal that weighs 150 to 200 pounds dressed. Any standard deer rifle will do. Because of the vastness of the western landscape, a scope-sighted rifle is highly recommended. The possibility of long shots also suggests you use something that can reach out with sufficient energy at extended yardages. I have no favorites, though my .30/06 has never failed me. Just make sure you can shoot whatever you shoot.

Trophies   Taking a record-class muley is a tough assignment because you'll have to look at and pass on plenty of marginal bucks, unless you're lucky and happen onto a trophy. Colorado is still the place to find a record, but don't overlook other states. Check these statistics when planning your hunt. Here's a breakdown, which includes listings from the B&C book.

Typical List (318 trophies)

Colorado	137
New Mexico	38
Idaho	33
Utah	29
Wyoming	25
Arizona	18
Montana	10
Oregon	8
Washington	5
British Columbia	4
Nevada	4
Saskatchewan	3
Mexico	2
Alberta	1
Unknown	1

Nontypical List (254 trophies)

Colorado	68
Idaho	36
Arizona	29
Utah	22
Montana	15
Wyoming	15
New Mexico	13
Saskatchewan	10
Oregon	9
Washington	9
Nevada	7
Alberta	5
British Columbia	5
California	3
Unknown	3
Nebraska	2
South Dakota	2
Kansas	1

1975–1980:

Colorado	14
Wyoming	4
Arizona	2
Idaho	1
New Mexico	1
Washington	1

Colorado	5
Arizona	1
Idaho	1
Wyoming	1

1980–1982:

Colorado 7	Colorado 9
Idaho 5	Arizona 4
Wyoming 5	Idaho 3
Oregon 3	Utah 3
Utah 3	Montana 2
Nevada 2	New Mexico 1
Alberta 1	Oregon 1
Arizona 1	Wyoming 1
British Columbia 1	
Montana 1	
New Mexico 1	
Saskatchewan 1	

Whitetail Deer

The West produces some surprisingly big whitetails, and every state that has them reports they're growing in number. They can be found on the fringes of agricultural areas, along stream and riverbottom vegetation, and in dense evergreen forests.

Hunting Tactics   The same techniques that work on eastern and southern whitetails work on these western deer. Watching scrapes and rubs, driving, hunting from tree stands, stillhunting, and other standard methods are effective.

Best States   Northeastern Washington has good whitetail hunting; in Idaho the best bet is in the panhandle. Montana has whitetails state-wide, Colorado's are in the northeast, and Wyoming's whitetails are in the north central and northeast regions.

Firearms   Any standard deer rifle will work for whitetails. If anything, the gun should be matched to the area hunted. Whitetail habitat varies widely; so does the weather, the average distance, and the visibility factor.

Trophies   The West isn't known for trophy whitetails, but Montana has been producing some good racks. The state ranks fourth for nontypical whitetails, eighth for typicals. Washington also has a good showing in the record book. As more hunters discover western whitetails, no doubt more trophies will surface. Here is data from the B&C record book.

Typical List (western heads)

Montana 19
Washington. 7
Colorado 2
Idaho .2
Wyoming. 1

Nontypical List

Montana 17
Washington. 14
Wyoming. 9
Idaho .4

1975–80:

Montana 5

Montana 2
Washington. 1

1980–1982:

Montana 2
Idaho .1
Washington. 1

III

A Look at the Western States

Arizona

Antelope Because Arizona has milder winters, as well as fewer hunters, than more northerly states, it is a top state for trophy antelope. A 16-inch buck is no eye-opener here, but it's rare in more popular antelope states. Anderson Mesa is one of the best areas. Between 800 and 1,000 tags are offered annually statewide, and a hunter success rate of around 70 percent and better is typical.

The season runs from late September to early October, lasting only a few days. A number of private ranches offer trophy hunting, but there is good hunting on BLM land as well.

Bighorn Sheep Arizona produces the biggest rams in the United States. The hunter success rate is generally better than 90 percent. About four dozen desert bighorn sheep tags are offered annually, and competition for the permits is intense. The hunting season runs for about two weeks in December.

Black Bear About 200 bears are taken by Arizona hunters annually. Many are killed in the spring, but fall hunts coincide with big-game

ARIZONA

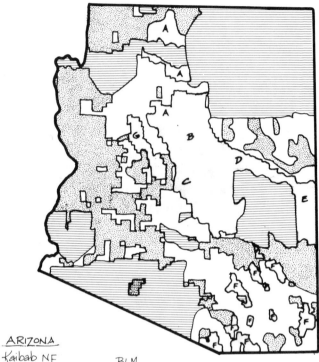

ARIZONA

A Kaibab NF
B Coconino NF
C Tonto NF
D Sitgreaves NF
E Apache NF
F Coronado NF
G Prescott NF

BLM
Arizona State Office
Phoenix, Arizona

Compiled by USGS, 1968
Scale 1:7,500,000

· FEDERAL LANDS ·

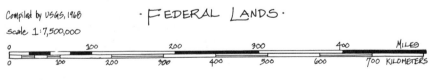

Bureau of Land Management   U.S. Forest Service   Other Federal Lands

seasons; a number of bears are taken incidentally by hunters pursuing deer and elk. Most seasons begin in late August and run to early December, but some units have different season schedules.

Deer   Arizona's deer herds are making a slow recovery from the severe decline of the 1970s. The Kaibab region bounced back after several years of low deer populations, and it is one of the bright spots in Arizona's program.

A lottery draw is required for deer permits, and competition is keen for Kaibab tags because huge bucks inhabit the region. The deadline for these and other deer permits is usually in late June. About 90,000 to 100,000 tags are offered annually. Many units are undersubscribed, and extra tags are sold after the drawing. As a rule, permits in the north are the toughest to get because there is much interest in the mule deer that live in the region.

Rocky Mountain muleys dwell in the area north of the Mogollon Rim; together with desert mule deer, they number about 200,000 animals. About 50,000 whitetails live in the south, and interest in hunting them isn't as high as in the north. There is generally no problem obtaining a whitetail tag in the south.

The total annual deer harvest runs between 15,000 and 20,000 animals, with a hunter success rate of around 20 percent. Rocky Mountain and desert mule deer make up the bulk of the harvest, with less than 5,000 being whitetails.

The general deer season runs from late October through December, but there are varying seasons in other units.

Elk   About 20,000 elk inhabit Arizona, most of them in the region from Flagstaff along the Mogollon Rim to the New Mexico border. This is a top state for elk, despite the comparatively low harvest. Between 2,000 and 3,000 elk are harvested each fall, with many of the bigger bulls coming from Indian reservations. However, national forests have produced some very big animals.

For trophy elk taken since 1970, Arizona ranks third in the Boone and Crockett record book, and many trophy hunters believe that a new world-record bull will come from this state.

Elk tags are offered in a lottery that has a late-June application deadline. Hunters can make two choices for areas. The general elk hunt runs from late November to early December. Bowhunters try for elk from mid-September to late September, and muzzleloader hunters go afield in late September.

Mountain Lion   This is a good mountain lion state, with an annual harvest consistently running about 200 animals. Some 2,000 big cats roam Arizona's deserts and mountains, and seasons are year-round in most of the state. The best counties include Cochise, Coconino, Gila, Graham, Greenlee, and Yavapai. Several first-class outfitters offer good hound hunts around the state. No lottery is required for a tag. For more information, contact the Arizona Game and Fish Department, 2222 W. Greenway Rd., Phoenix, AZ 85023 (602-942-3000).

California

Antelope California has a static antelope herd, with a population of about 7,000 animals, most of which live in the northeast region. Each year, about 600 permits are offered. Hunter success is high, running about 90 percent, and trophy bucks are not uncommon. The lottery deadline is in early July; only residents may hunt.

Black Bear Some 700 to 1,000 black bears are taken by hunters annually. Spring hunting and baiting are prohibited. Most bears are taken by hunters with hound packs, and the season runs in November and December. Best bear hunting is in the mountains in the northern half of the state. Much of the hunting is on national forests.

Deer All of California's deer management units are on a quota basis; quotas vary each year because of herd fluctuations and management priorities. This intensive program is expected to improve California's deer hunting. The state has the poorest hunter success rate in the West, with rates running from 7 to 10 percent. The best hunting is on private land, and the top areas are generally leased to sportsman's clubs or groups of hunters. About 300,000 deer tags are sold annually, with a harvest of about 25,000 to 30,000 deer. In the A zones, seasons open in mid-August, while other seasons open in September and October. Bow seasons are usually held prior to the general firearms season, and muzzleloader hunts occur after the general seasons. In some units, two bucks may be taken.

Blacktails and several mule deer species inhabit California. Popular among hunters, Rocky Mountain muleys dwell in the northeast. Some units in this region are hunted only by winning a permit in a highly competitive lottery. Hunter success is very good, usually 50 percent and better.

Wild Hog Hogs are second only to deer in California, and are hunted

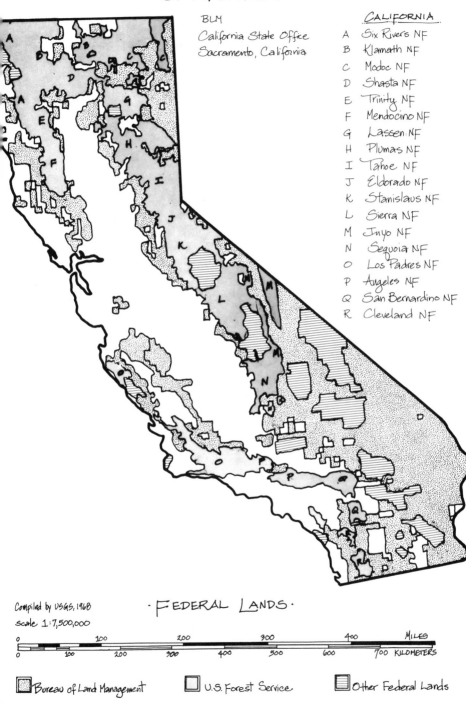

CALIFORNIA

BLM
California State Office
Sacramento, California

CALIFORNIA

A Six Rivers NF
B Klamath NF
C Modoc NF
D Shasta NF
E Trinity NF
F Mendocino NF
G Lassen NF
H Plumas NF
I Tahoe NF
J Eldorado NF
K Stanislaus NF
L Sierra NF
M Inyo NF
N Sequoia NF
O Los Padres NF
P Angeles NF
Q San Bernardino NF
R Cleveland NF

· FEDERAL LANDS ·

Compiled by USGS, 1968
Scale 1:7,500,000

| 0 | 100 | 200 | 300 | 400 | MILES |

| 0 | 100 | 200 | 300 | 400 | 500 | 600 | 700 KILOMETERS |

▢ Bureau of Land Management   ▢ U.S. Forest Service   ▢ Other Federal Lands

year-round. Most hunting is on private land, and a general license is required to hunt them.

For more information, contact the Department of Fish and Game, 1416 Ninth St., Sacramento, CA 95814 (916-323-3891).

Colorado

Antelope   Colorado's antelope are thriving, but some herds will take some time to recover from severe winters in the mid 1980s, chiefly in the area north of Craig. This is also Colorado's best antelope region; it holds the biggest bucks in the state. Between 40,000 and 50,000 antelope live in Colorado, and about 15,000 tags are issued annually in a lottery. Plenty of public land is available for hunters. The rifle antelope season is in late September; the bowhunting opener is mid-August.

Bighorn Sheep   Some 5,000 Rocky Mountain bighorns dwell in Colorado, and about 400 tags are issued each year. Recently, nonresident permits were made available. The application deadline for the lottery is in late April. In some areas, ewe-only seasons are held to keep herds at healthy levels. Bowhunters take some very big rams; this state is often ranked high in the Pope & Young record book for bighorns.

Black Bear   About 700 to 800 bears have been harvested annually for the last several seasons. One of the most liberal western states for bear hunting, Colorado allows spring hunting, baiting, and hunting with hounds. The spring hunts usually run from April 1 to some time in June. Fall seasons vary with the unit. Bear hunting is good in the western mountains, and there is plenty of public hunting on national forest lands.

Deer   Colorado is a top mule deer state, and the record book clearly shows it to be the best for trophy deer. Herds number close to a half million deer, and numbers fluctuate widely because of winterkill. Though there is good hunting on national forests in the western mountains, some of the best hunting is on private lands. Practically all are leased by hunter groups.

Crowds are typical on public land during general seasons, because hunting is unlimited and there is no control on hunter pressure. Hunters who work hard can still take very good bucks on public land. Trophies come from throughout the west slope; most hunters do best by penetrating areas far from access roads. Whitetails are thriving in the east, with

COLORADO

COLORADO

A Routt NF
B Roosevelt NF
C Arapaho NF
D White NF
E Pike NF
F Grand Mesa NF
G Gunnison NF
H Uncompahgre NF
I San Juan NF
J Rio Grande NF
K San Isabel NF

BLM
Colorado State Office
Denver, Colorado

Compiled by USGS, 1968
scale 1:7,500,000

· FEDERAL LANDS ·

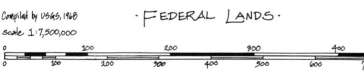

⬛ Bureau of Land Management   ⬜ U.S. Forest Service   ▤ Other Federal Lands

good populations along the South Platte River, and along other brushy drainages.

Deer seasons are split; a deer-only early season begins in late October, and a combined deer-elk season starts in early November. Tags are unlimited.

Elk   Colorado has the distinction of having more elk than other western states, and it also yields the most elk compared to other states. However, it also has the most hunters, and for that reason, mature bulls are scarce in many units.

Heavy hunter pressure due to unlimited permits has been a major factor in overharvesting bulls. There are recent changes in the hunting rules that will help the situation. In some major hunting areas, only four-point bulls are legal, and this regulation is expected to be instituted in most herd units in the future. In addition, Colorado has 20 limited-entry units where a lottery draw is required to obtain a tag. In these units, hunters are restricted, and success rates are higher. More bulls escape each year as well, and a quality hunt is the result. An early elk-only season starts in mid-October, a later combined elk-deer season starts in early November.

Moose   Wyoming moose were transplanted into Colorado in the late 1970s, and the herd has grown to the point where a few tags are offered annually to residents only. All the moose are in the North Park area near Walden.

Mountain Goat   Goat populations are steadily increasing, and more and more tags are offered each year. About 100 tags are offered annually, and nonresidents have recently been allowed to hunt. Hunter success runs about 80 percent.

Mountain Lion   Between 100 and 150 lions are taken annually from a population believed to number about 1,000 animals. Lions are managed on a quota system. Quotas are set for each management unit; when the quota is reached hunting is terminated for the season. Tags can be purchased anytime, provided quotas have not been reached. Lions are hunted throughout the western mountains.

For more information, contact the Colorado Division of Wildlife, 6060 Broadway, Denver, CO 80216 (303-297-1192).

Idaho

Antelope About 2,500 antelope are harvested annually from a herd of approximately 20,000 in the state. Hunter success rates are 75 to 80 percent, and public land offers excellent hunting opportunities. Tags must be obtained in a drawing; the application deadline is late June. Seasons vary, but the earliest opens about the third week in August.

Bighorn Sheep There are some fine bighorn sheep herds in Idaho, with tags offered to residents and nonresidents each year. Most sheep are in rough country, requiring an outfitter or backwoods experience. The season varies, but opens late August in most units.

Black Bear Idaho is one of the top western states for black bears, with an annual harvest approaching 1,000. Bear populations are so high in some areas that a two-bear limit is allowed. Bears kill significant numbers of calf elk, which is the reason for the two-bear limit. Most bruins are taken in the spring, but a number of bears are killed in the fall, as well. Bear tags are unlimited and can be purchased without a lottery drawing. The Selway and Salmon river drainages are among Idaho's finest bear areas.

Deer Idaho has a large mule deer herd, and whitetails are doing very well. Most muleys inhabit central and southern Idaho, while whitetails are in the panhandle. This state is attaining notoriety for trophy-class mule deer, particularly in the southeast region. Bucks with 30-inch racks are frequently taken by hunters who work hard and get into the backcountry. Trophy whitetails are also reported around the fertile panhandle farmlands as well as in densely timbered forests in the north. Plenty of national forests allow public hunting throughout the state.

Resident deer tags are unlimited, and 11,500 tags are reserved for nonresidents on a first-come basis. Deer seasons vary, with some seasons opening as early as mid-September, but these are chiefly in backcountry units. Most general seasons open in October. Nonresident tags sell out earlier and earlier each year; it's wise to apply for an application as soon as they're available.

Elk Idaho's elk herds went through a severe decline recently, but are now making a dramatic recovery. This is due to intense elk management programs, as well as habitat improvement. Idaho can now be considered one of the best elk states in the West, a distinction that couldn't have been possible just ten years ago. Elk range throughout most for-

IDAHO

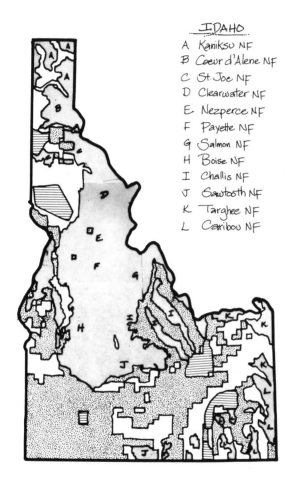

IDAHO

A Kaniksu NF
B Coeur d'Alene NF
C St. Joe NF
D Clearwater NF
E Nezperce NF
F Payette NF
G Salmon NF
H Boise NF
I Challis NF
J Sawtooth NF
K Targhee NF
L Caribou NF

BLM
Idaho State Office,
Boise, Idaho

· FEDERAL LANDS ·

Compiled by USGS, 1968
scale 1:7,500,000

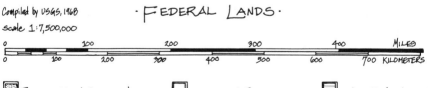

Bureau of Land Management   U.S. Forest Service   Other Federal Lands

ested areas, and are toughest to hunt in the thick Panhandle timberlands. The vast Selway Wilderness Area is a prime spot, with high populations and plenty of big bulls.

As a result of the exploding elk herds, extra nonresident elk tags have recently been offered in addition to the regular quota of about 10,000. Tags are available on a first-come basis, and, like deer, sell out more quickly each year. Resident tags are unlimited. The general elk season begins September 15 in some units, later in others.

Moose   There are about 300 moose permits available each fall, and hunters achieve a success rate of about 90 percent. There would be more moose tags in Idaho, but poaching has been responsible for more conservative quotas. About 5,000 moose live in the state, with herds scattered from the Panhandle to forests south of the Salmon River. Only Idaho residents may hunt moose.

Mountain Goat   About 60 goat tags are issued each year in Idaho. Hunter success runs about 70 to 75 percent. Goat units are high and rugged, requiring plenty of preparation before making a hunt. An outfitter is strongly advised if you are to have a successful hunt. You'll need to be in good physical condition to try a hunt on your own, with plenty of backwoods experience. Seasons begin August 31 and vary according to the unit.

Mountain Lion   This is one of the best cougar states; upwards of 200 animals are taken annually. Hunting seasons vary according to the unit. Some run well into winter, while others occur during the fall deer and elk seasons. A drawing is not required for a lion tag. The season opens August 31 in many units and often runs as late as the end of March.

For more information, contact the Idaho Fish and Game Department, 600 S. Walnut, Box 25, Boise, ID 83707 (208-334-3700).

Montana

Antelope   Montana is second only to Wyoming in antelope populations and annual harvest. Between 35,000 and 40,000 animals are taken annually. Most antelope seasons begin in mid-October and mid-November, with trophy-class bucks taken in all the regions where antelope are hunted. Plenty of public land is available, but much hunting is on private land. The deadline for lottery applications is June 1.

Bighorn Sheep   Montana is the only state that offers unlimited Rocky Mountain bighorn sheep tags. Hunters may buy a tag for selected units

The author with a fine bull he took in Idaho. Of the Rocky Mountain states, Colorado, Montana, Idaho, and Wyoming are tops for elk. Each of them produces a harvest of at least 10,000 elk annually. They're also excellent for other big game, especially mule deer.

MONTANA

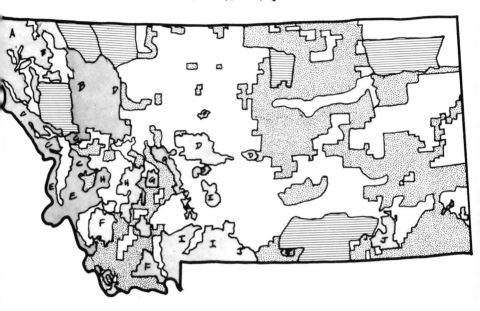

MONTANA

A Kootenai NF
B Flathead NF
C Lolo NF
D Lewis & Clark NF
E Bitterroot NF
F Beaverhead NF
G Helena NF
H Deerlodge NF
I Gallatin NF
J Custer NF

BLM
Montana State Office
Billings, Montana

Compiled by USGS, 1968

scale 1:7,500,000

· FEDERAL LANDS ·

0   100   200   300   400   MILES

0   100   200   300   400   500   600   700 KILOMETERS

▦ Bureau of Land Management   ☐ U.S. Forest Service   ▤ Other Federal Lands

but, once the quota is reached, the season is terminated. Hunter success is very low in these units. Access is difficult, and the regions are extremely rugged. A number of ewe tags are made available in order to maintain healthy sheep populations. These, and most sheep permits, are offered in a lottery draw. Most sheep seasons start September 15, and the application deadline is June 1. About 300 limited tags are offered annually.

Black Bear   Montana has a large population of black bears, and also has the most restrictive hunting regulations. While hunters can use bait or hounds, or both, in most other western states, Montana allows neither. All hunting must be done by spotting bears in their natural environment. About 1,500 bears are taken annually, the bulk of them in the fall, and usually by hunters pursuing deer and elk.

Deer   Montana's deer populations are high in most regions, with excellent hunting opportunities for both muleys and whitetails. The harvest has reached 150,000 deer in recent years. Whitetails are the biggest news in this state. They're increasing in number each year, and trophy bucks are being taken from around the state, chiefly in the northwest region. Whitetails are hunted in dense forests in the west, and along riverbottoms in central and eastern Montana. Much of the land is private in the east, but landowners are often willing to allow hunting. Mule deer are hunted everywhere, but the southwest region is most popular. Trophy-class muleys aren't easy to come by, but there are plenty of respectable bucks in many units.

Montana offers unlimited tags to residents, and a quota of 17,000 combination tags to nonresidents. The combination tag allows an elk, deer, black bear, birds, and fish. There are also A and B deer tags, which are available in a lottery drawing. The combination tag, normally sold on a first-come basis, may be eliminated because of intense competition among nonresidents. Most A tags are for bucks only; B tags are antlerless. Deer seasons vary with the unit, but most open late October and run to late November.

Elk   There is a moderately increasing elk population in the state, with hunting good to excellent in most regions. The general elk firearms season runs from late October to December, but there are early seasons in some backcountry areas including the Bob Marshall, Absaroka-Beartooth, Great Bear, and Lincoln-Scapegoat wilderness areas. The season opens September 15 in these areas, and hunters can try for bulls during the breeding period. Because of the remoteness of these areas, outfitters are advised.

Montana has the distinction of producing more record-class bulls than any other state. Some 15,000 animals are harvested annually, many of them large mature bulls. Two late hunts in the Gardiner and Gallatin areas give up big elk each year. In both areas, elk migrating out of Yellowstone Park are harvested. A lottery draw is required to obtain a tag, and the computer assigns the hunt period, which may be two or four days. Hunts start in early December and run through late February. There are other excellent limited-entry permits in the state.

Astute hunters often hold off their hunting efforts until the last week of the general season, which is in late November. Deep snow drives elk out of the high country, and migrating elk are available to hunters in the lower elevations as the animals head for winter ranges.

Resident elk tags are unlimited; nonresidents must buy a tag on a first-come basis, but, as explained above, the system may change.

Grizzly Bear Unlimited numbers of grizzly tags are sold, and the season continues until a limited quota is reached. Montana is the only state in the lower 48 to offer grizzly bear hunting, and hunter success is very low when compared to Alaska and Canada.

Moose About 600 tags are offered in five regions. The best hunting is around Yellowstone Park and the western and southwestern areas. Seasons begin September 15 in most units. Hunter success is high, generally 80 percent or better.

Mountain Goat The goat population is in good shape, with about 350 permits offered each year. The best hunting is in the Bitterroot Range along the western border. The season usually runs September 15 to December 1.

Mountain Lion Lion populations are stable in Montana, with an annual harvest of about 100 animals. Tags are unlimited, but they must be purchased prior to August 31 each year. The season runs from early December to mid-February each year.

For more information, contact the Montana Department of Fish, Wildlife, and Parks, 1420 E. Sixth, Helena, MT 59620 (406-444-2535).

Nevada

Antelope Because of increasing populations, Nevada has been offering more antelope tags each year. Almost 700 tags are available, and recently some nonresident permits were allotted. Some of the best hunt-

NEVADA

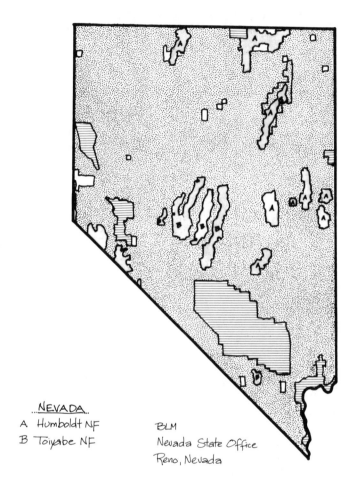

<u>NEVADA</u>

A Humboldt NF
B Toiyabe NF

BLM
Nevada State Office
Reno, Nevada

Compiled by USGS, 1968
scale 1:7,500,000

· FEDERAL LANDS ·

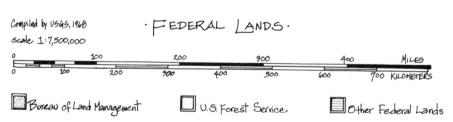

Bureau of Land Management   U.S. Forest Service   Other Federal Lands

ing is on the Sheldon Game Range, which is known for trophy-class antelope. Hunter success is high, running better than 80 percent. Although Nevada isn't well known as an antelope state, the restricted hunts allow bucks to grow old and attain large horns. Two seasons are held each year, both starting in August.

Bighorn Sheep   Nevada has long been known for desert bighorns but Rocky Mountain bighorns have recently been added to the hunt list. California bighorns are also hunted. About 120 desert bighorn, and three each Rocky Mountain and California bighorn tags are offered annually. Competition is tough for tags, especially for desert sheep tags among nonresidents. Season dates for Rocky Mountain and California bighorn sheep are early September to early October. The season for desert bighorn sheep is mid-November to mid-December.

Deer   Residents and nonresidents alike must draw deer tags in a lottery, and about 20,000 tags are annually offered. This is exclusively a Rocky Mountain mule deer state, with excellent hunting. Many hunters see Nevada as a barren place devoid of wildlife, but it has plenty of prime deer country in several mountainous regions.

The areas around Elko are the most popular and the toughest to draw, but some of the biggest bucks come from the central region. Because hunter pressure is restricted, many bucks escape and grow mature antlers. Hunter success in Nevada is very good, usually well above 50 percent. A good share of the bucks harvested are mature four-pointers.

The application deadline for tags is early July; each hunter is allowed to apply for five areas. The season usually starts in early October and runs almost a month, giving hunters plenty of time to find a good buck. Snow is usually present during the latter part of the season in upper elevations, allowing hunters an advantage of tracking deer and seeing them more readily.

Elk   About 50 bull tags and some cow tags are offered to residents only. Elk are increasing in Nevada, and a few herds are hunted on a very limited basis. Hunter success is extremely high, usually better than 90 percent. One of the best spots for big bulls is the Pilot Peak area on the Utah border. This is a rugged mountain, but it contains huge elk, and has just recently been hunted. There are two elk seasons, one beginning in late September, the other mid-November.

Mountain Goat   A few mountain goat tags are issued every other year or so. Only residents may hunt them. A small herd lives in the Ruby Mountains near Elko.

Mountain Lion   Tags are unlimited, but the hunter must select a unit. Hunts are held on a quota system. When the quota is reached in that unit, the area is closed. Several regions have good lion populations, but White Pine County is one of the best. Seasons vary according to the unit.

For more information, contact the Nevada Department of Wildlife, Box 10678, Reno, NV 89520 (702-789-0500).

New Mexico

Antelope   This is one of the top antelope states in terms of trophies, with some 3,000 permits offered each year. Hunter success is about 80 percent; seasons run two or three days depending on the region. A lottery drawing is required to hunt antelope on public land, but landowners are issued tags by the state and are allowed to allocate them to whomever they choose. The application deadline is late June.

Bighorn Sheep   About a dozen tags are offered each year to residents and nonresidents. There are two hunts: one in the Pecos River area in September, and one in the San Francisco Mountains in January. Application deadline is late June.

Black Bear   About 400 bears are harvested annually in the state. Besides the spring hunt, which runs from mid-May to mid-June, a hunt from mid-August to mid-December is held as well. Bear tags are unlimited.

Deer   New Mexico's deer herds are gradually improving, and are building nicely after the west-wide mule deer decline of the 1970s. Mule deer, Texas whitetails, and Coues whitetails inhabit the state. New Mexico offers stratified deer hunts, which run two, five, and seven days. A hunter may choose only one hunt.

The northern counties traditionally produce the biggest bucks, especially backcountry areas of the Carson National Forest. The Valle Vidal Unit opened recently and offers very good mule deer hunting. This area was once part of the famous Vermejo Park and was donated to the government. It has been incorporated into the Carson National Forest, and a lottery draw is required in order to obtain a tag.

The southern region has Texas and Coues whitetails, but interest in

NEW MEXICO

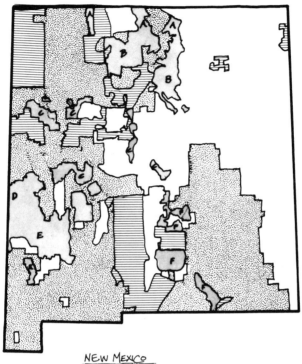

NEW MEXICO

A Carson NF
B Santa Fe NF
C Cibola NF
D Apache NF
E Gila NF
F Lincoln NF

BLM
New Mexico State Office
Santa Fe, New Mexico

Compiled by USGS, 1968
Scale 1:7,500,000

· FEDERAL LANDS ·

 Bureau of Land Management   ☐ U.S. Forest Service   ☰ Other Federal Lands

them is not as high as it is for northern muleys. Between 25,000 and 30,000 deer are taken annually, with hunter success running around 25 to 30 percent.

Elk   About 2,000 elk are harvested annually in New Mexico. This state is well known for the large ranches that offer quality hunting. The hunts are higher priced than most, but the odds of taking a trophy-class bull are greater than in most other areas. In order to hunt public land, hunters must draw a tag in a lottery. Several national forests offer good hunting. The application deadline for elk tags is mid-July. The Valle Vidal Unit, mentioned above, offers very good elk hunting, but competition is high for tags.

Mountain Lion   About 100 mountain lions are taken each year, chiefly in the Black Range, Burro, Gila, and Sangre de Cristo mountains. This is a top lion state, with an estimated 2,000 big cats roaming about. The statewide season runs from December 1 to March 31.

Oryx, Ibex, Barbary Sheep   Many years ago, several areas were stocked with these exotic big game animals. They're thriving in many areas, with tags awarded in a lottery. Some animals are so plentiful that tags are easy to obtain. Seasons vary according to species and the unit they live in.

For more information, contact the New Mexico Game and Fish Department, Villagra Bldg., Santa Fe, NM 87503 (505-827-7911).

Oregon

Antelope   About 1,400 tags are offered annually, and hunters take about 1,000 antelope. Hunter success runs about 60 percent each year. Hunts are a week long, and are held in mid-August. Private land offers some of the best hunting, but public hunting is available on BLM lands. The application deadline is in early May.

Bighorn Sheep   There are about 50 sheep permits offered annually, mostly for California bighorns in the southeast. A half dozen or so Rocky Mountain bighorn tags are available in the northeast region. The season starts in mid-September; only residents can hunt.

Black Bear   Oregon is a top bear state, with more than 1,000 taken each year. Most are killed incidentally by hunters who are after deer and elk. The season runs from late August to late November, and tags are unlimited.

OREGON

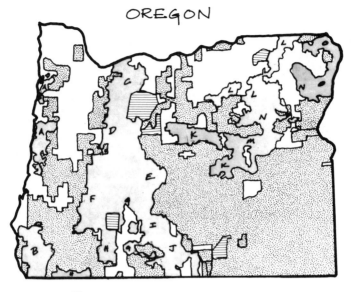

OREGON

A Siuslaw NF
B Siskiyou NF
C Mt. Hood NF
D Willamette NF
E Deschutes NF
F Umpqua NF
G Winema NF
H Rogue River NF
I Klamath NF
J Fremont NF
K Ochoco NF
L Umatilla NF
M Malheur NF
N Whitman NF
O Wallowa NF

BLM
Oregon State Office,
Portland, Oregon

· FEDERAL LANDS ·

Compiled by USGS, 1968
Scale 1:7,500,000

| 0 | 100 | 200 | 300 | 400 | MILES |

| 0 | 100 | 200 | 300 | 400 | 500 | 600 | 700 KILOMETERS |

▨ Bureau of Land Management   ☐ U.S. Forest Service   ▤ Other Federal Lands

Deer   Oregon offers hunting for Rocky Mountain mule deer and black-tails. The former dwell in the eastern region, which is arid and similar to the west, while the latter inhabit the West Coast mountain range from the Cascade Mountains to the ocean. Rocky Mountain mule deer in the east number about 250,000. Some 100,000 or so hunters try for them each year, and take about 30,000 animals. About 450,000 blacktails dwell in western forests; some 40,000 to 50,000 are taken by 150,000 hunters annually. The mule deer is the more popular quarry, but more blacktails are taken because most of Oregon's hunters live in blacktail range. Deer hunts begin in late September. Muley hunts run less than two weeks; some blacktail seasons extend into November.

Deer tags are unlimited, but there are some limited-entry permits that require a lottery draw. The Steens Mountains region offers one of the best limited entry hunts. Some antlerless tags are offered in the east where population control is required, and in isolated areas where deer are causing damage.

Elk   About 15,000 elk are taken from Oregon each year, ranking this state among the best in the West in terms of elk harvest. Good bulls are difficult to find, however, because of heavy hunter pressure in prime elk country. Spikes often make up the major part of the bull harvest in many areas. The population trends are up, however, and elk are increasing in number in many areas.

Rocky Mountain elk live in the east, while Roosevelt elk inhabit the mountains from the Cascade Range west to the coast. Hunters generally prefer to hunt the east region because it's more open and hunting isn't as difficult as in the thick timber of the western forests.

Elk seasons begin anywhere from late October to mid-November, depending on the species and unit. Elk tags are unlimited, and there are some very good quality units where a lottery draw selects hunters. In some areas, spikes are protected.

Mountain Lion   Each year, about 50 lions are taken by some 200 or so hunters. In western Oregon, the season generally starts in early December and runs two months; in the east it runs throughout December. Permits must be applied for in a lottery that has an early May application deadline.

For more information, contact the Oregon Department of Fish and Wildlife, Box 3503, Portland, OR 97208. (503-229-5551).

Utah

Antelope　The antelope herd in Utah is slowly increasing, with about 6,000 animals currently inhabiting the state. Hunter success runs about 85 to 90 percent each year; some 500 animals are harvested annually. Recent transplant programs have been responsible for establishing new herds and increasing others. Licenses are offered in a computer drawing, with a late July application deadline. A few tags are offered to nonresidents. Hunts are held in September.

Black Bear　Less than 50 black bears are taken in Utah each year, and there is limited interest in hunting them. However, Utah gave up the No. 1 and No. 2 black bears as listed in the Boone and Crockett record book. Spring and fall seasons are held. Hunting with hounds is legal, but the use of baits is prohibited for all but bowhunters. The Book Cliffs area in the northeast is the top spot, but there are some very big bears in the central mountain ranges.

Bighorn Sheep　Utah offers about a dozen or so desert bighorn sheep tags each year, sometimes one or two to nonresidents. The sheep country is extremely difficult to hunt, especially if bighorns are deep in the rugged canyons. Hunter success fluctuates. Some years it's less than 20 percent, others it's better than 75 percent.

Buffalo　Utah has one of the only truly wild buffalo herds in North America. These animals dwell in the Henry Mountains, and they are tough to hunt. About 25 to 45 permits are offered each year, depending on the size of the herd. A few tags are offered to nonresidents.

Deer　Between 60,000 and 80,000 deer are taken annually by hunters in Utah. This is exclusively a mule deer state, with upwards of half a million deer. Herds are scattered throughout the state, but the best hunting is in the central, northern, and northeast mountain areas. During severe winters, herds in the north are hard hit and substantial dieoffs occur. Two new limited-entry areas that provide superb hunting are the San Juan-Elk Ridge and Pine Valley units in the south.

The general deer hunt begins in mid-October and runs for 11 days. The bowhunt starts in mid-August; muzzleloader hunting usually starts after the general season ends. Deer tags for the general hunt are unlimited and can be purchased from license vendors before or during the season.

UTAH

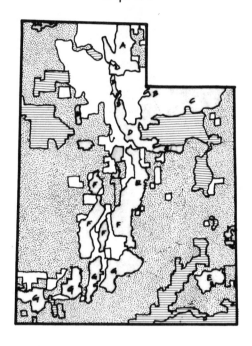

UTAH

A Cache NF
B Wasatch NF
C Ashley, NF
D Uinta NF
E Manti-La Sal NF
F Fishlake NF
G Dixie NF

BLM
Utah State Office
Salt Lake City, Utah

Compiled by USGS, 1968
scale 1:7,500,000

· FEDERAL LANDS ·

| 0 | 100 | 200 | 300 | 400 | MILES |

| 0 | 100 | 200 | 300 | 400 | 500 | 600 | 700 | KILOMETERS |

 Bureau of Land Management   ▢ U.S. Forest Service   ▤ Other Federal Lands

Elk   Elk herds in Utah have been nothing to brag about in the past, but times are changing. With about 25,000 elk roaming the state and rapidly increasing herds, good hunting is not far off. There are 31 elk units in Utah, and new ones open each year. There are many limited-entry areas that require a drawing for a tag. These units offer high hunter success rates and an excellent chance of taking a fine bull. Wildlife officials have been transplanting elk within the state. Excess animals are trapped from Hardware Ranch, where the Division of Wildlife Resources feeds elk in the winter, and are stocked in places that have no elk or have only small herds that need to be strengthened.

Elk herds are now scattered in mountain ranges around Utah, with good populations in all regions. The season usually runs from early to mid-October and coincides with the breeding period, but heavy hunting pressure on public land often stymies bugling efforts. Tags are unlimited for residents and nonresidents, but they must be purchased prior to the season's opening day. The application deadline for limited entry permits is in late July.

Moose   About 100 moose tags are offered each year, with a few available to nonresidents. Utah's moose populations are stable to increasing; all hunting is in the northern half of the state. Several national forests offer public access, but some of the best hunting is on private land. Seasons vary with the unit; they open in September and November.

Mountain Goat   There are a few goat tags available each year to resident hunters. Utah opened its first season a few years ago. All the goats dwell in the steep, rugged mountains of the Wasatch Range adjacent to the Salt Lake area.

Mountain Lion   Some 150 to 200 lions are harvested annually in Utah. Populations are stable to increasing in most areas, with the best hunting in the southwest. The season varies, but the general hunt runs from January to August in many regions. Several outfitters with hound packs offer lion hunting. The long season allows a unique lion/bear combination hunt in some regions because seasons overlap.

For more information, contact the Utah Division of Wildlife Resources, 1596 West North Temple, Salt Lake City, UT 84116 (801-533-9333).

Washington

Bighorn Sheep There are about 600 California bighorns and 100 Rocky Mountain bighorns in Washington. About a dozen tags are offered to hunters. Hunts are held in the Vulcan, Murray, and Umtanum areas, with most permits set aside for bowhunters and a few for rifle and muzzleloader hunters. Dates vary with the hunts and methods used.

Black Bear Black bear populations are somewhat stabilized and are slowly on the way up. In the 1940s and 1950s, bear numbers were double what they are now, and bears were causing extensive damage to young commercial trees by stripping the bark and killing the trees. Control programs were responsible for heavy bear harvests, and now the population is as low as it's ever been. Conservative seasons are now allowing bears to maintain their populations and inch back up. In 1981, wildlife officials cut the bear season from seven to three months. Now, about 2,000 bears are taken each year, most of them in September and October, prior to deer season. Bear tags are unlimited.

Deer Washington is the only western state to offer good hunting opportunities for three species of deer: blacktails, Rocky Mountain mule deer, and whitetails. Blacktails live in the western mountains from the Cascade Range west to the ocean. Rocky Mountain muleys live in the eastern region, and whitetails dwell in the northeast area.

The state has been offering more bowhunting and muzzleloading opportunities in order to draw some rifle hunters from the general firearms season into the primitive weapons seasons, thus reducing crowding during the general hunt. A hunter may select only one method of hunting, whether he is successful or not.

A harvest of approximately 40,000 deer is typical. That includes about 20,000 blacktails, 13,000 mule deer, and 7,000 whitetails. Tags are unlimited for the general firearms hunt, but there are antlerless tags available in a lottery. The application deadline is in early August. Seasons vary according to the unit, but the general hunt begins in October.

Elk Both Roosevelt and Rocky Mountain elk live in Washington. The former live in the mountains from the Cascade Range to the ocean; the latter live in eastern Washington. About 10,000 elk are harvested each year. Hunting seasons vary with the area; they start in late October and in early November. The early hunts are the most popular because elk

WASHINGTON

WASHINGTON

A Olympic NF
B Mt. Baker NF
C Okanogan NF
D Colville NF
E Wenatchee NF
F. Snoqualmie NF
G Gifford Pinchot NF

BLM
Oregon State Office
Portland, Oregon

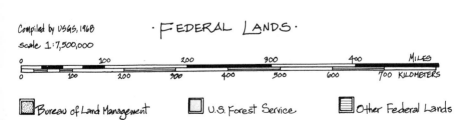

Compiled by USGS, 1968
Scale 1:7,500,000

· FEDERAL LANDS ·

						MILES
0	100	200	300	400		
0	100	200	300	400	500	600	700 KILOMETERS

Bureau of Land Management   U.S. Forest Service   Other Federal Lands

haven't been disturbed. Those who buy an early-season tag can hunt only bulls; hunters purchasing a late-season tag may apply for a special antlerless or branch-antlered bull permit. General tags are unlimited.

Moose A few tags are given each year for the small moose herd in the Selkirk Mountains. Competition is keen for the tags because several thousand hunters apply for them. Hunter success is normally very high.

Mountain Lion The lion population is stable, and the seasons vary depending on the region. Tags are currently unlimited. Nonresident hunters must buy lion tags 14 days in advance of the hunt. Seasons vary according to the unit.

Mountain Goat This is one of the best mountain goat states in the lower 48. Hunts are more conservative than usual; in 1970, there were 1,000 permits available; now, there are fewer than 300 offered. Goat habitat is being lost to roads, and more accurate inventory techniques allow for better means of counting animals. The season generally runs the entire month of October in most units.

For more information, contact the Washington Department of Game, 600 N. Capitol Way, Olympia WA 98504 (206-753-5700).

Wyoming

Antelope More than 100,000 antelope tags are offered each year, with hunts in every part of the state except high mountain ranges. Permits are offered in a lottery, but so many are left over after the drawing it's no problem to obtain one. In many units, it's possible to buy one or more additional tags, which must be antlerless. After opening day, these tags are sold at half price. Some units have unlimited numbers of tags per hunter until a quota is reached. Upwards of 75,000 to 90,000 antelope are harvested annually. Biggest bucks come from the south central region. Antelope seasons vary according to the unit, but most open in September and October and run for two weeks or more.

Bighorn Sheep About 6,000 Rocky Mountain bighorns inhabit the state; about 150 to 175 are harvested annually for a hunter success rate of 50 to 60 percent. Some of the best sheep hunting is in the Cody and Jackson areas, but there are big rams in the Medicine Bow region near Encampment, and scattered herds dwell in mountains throughout the central area as well.

WYOMING

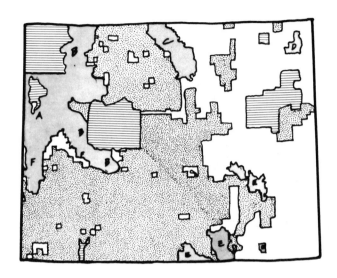

WYOMING.

A Teton NF
B Shoshone NF
C Bighorn NF
D Black Hills NF (So Data)
E Medicine Bow NF
F Bridger NF

BLM
Wyoming State Office,
Cheyenne, Wyoming

Compiled by USGS, 1968
scale 1:7,500,000

· FEDERAL LANDS ·

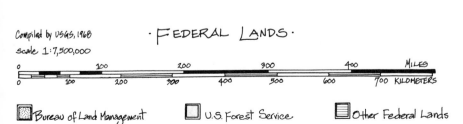

Bureau of Land Management   U.S. Forest Service   Other Federal Lands

Black Bear   About 200 bears are taken each year, with most harvested in the spring. Hounds are prohibited, but baiting is allowed except for units around Yellowstone Park where grizzlies live. Teton and Sublette counties are among the best for black bears, but hunting is good in most of the western mountain ranges as well as the Bighorn Mountains. Seasons vary according to the unit.

Deer   Mule deer are well represented in Wyoming, with herds scattered around the state from prairie deserts to high country regions. The Rocky Mountain mule deer is the most popular, but a whitetail herd is rapidly expanding its range westward across Wyoming. The best whitetail hunting is in the northeast and north central regions. Trophy-class muleys are not uncommon in the state; most come from the Bridger-Teton National Forest in the western mountains. In many units, it's possible to combine a mule deer and antelope hunt.

Wyoming resident tags are unlimited; nonresidents must apply in a lottery with a traditional March 15 application deadline. Tags are tough to get in the best regions. Each year, some tags are left over after the drawing, chiefly in the northeast region inhabited by whitetails.

Elk   About 65,000 elk inhabit Wyoming after the hunting season; average harvest is about 15,000 animals with a success rate of about 30 percent. Herds are stable to increasing, and seasons are long in many units, running from mid-September to late November. In some areas, spike bulls are protected. Nonresidents must apply for a tag in a lottery that traditionally has a February 1 deadline. Unsuccessful nonresidents can buy elk tags on a first-come basis in July, if any are left over after the resident tags are allotted. Usually, about 1,000 extra tags are available.

Trophy elk come from various parts of the state, but some of the biggest are taken from areas adjacent to Yellowstone Park as well as the Wyoming range. Seasons vary with the unit, and some backcountry units allow rifle hunting during the rut period. October 15 is a common opening date in many units, and there are some very late hunts in Teton National Park and the National Elk Refuge.

Moose   This is the top state for Wyoming, or Shira's, moose, with a population of about 8,000. About 1,000 moose are killed annually, with a hunter success rate of 85 percent or so. The western mountains are inhabited by moose, with some of the biggest in the Pinedale/Jackson area. Seasons vary with the unit; they run from mid-September into November.

Mountain Goat   Less than a dozen goat tags are issued annually. Hunter success is about 100 percent. The odds of drawing a tag are about one in 200 for residents, one in 30 for nonresidents.

Mountain Lion   About 50 lions are taken in Wyoming each year. Most come from the Bighorn Mountains, and there are also good populations in the Cody area from Meteetse to Clarks Fork. Seasons vary with the unit.

For more information, contact the Wyoming Game and Fish Department, Cheyenne, WY 82002 (307-777-7735).

IV

Appendix

Arizona

National Forests in Arizona

Apache-Sitgreaves National Forest, Federal Bldg., P.O. Box 640, Springerville, AZ 85938 (602-333-4301).

Coconino National Forest, 2323 E. Greenlaw Lane, Flagstaff, AZ 86001 (602-779-3311).

Coronado National Forest, 301 W. Congress, P.O. Box 551, Tucson, AZ 85702 (602-792-6483).

Kaibab National Forest, 800 S. Sixth St., Williams, AZ 86046 (602-635-2681).

Prescott National Forest, 344 S. Cortez, P.O. Box 2549, Prescott, AZ 86031 (602-445-1762).

Tonto National Forest, 102 S. 28th St., P.O. Box 29070, Phoenix, AZ 85038 (602-261-3205).

Bureau of Land Management: Arizona State Office, 2400 Valley Bank Center, Phoenix, AZ 85073 (602-261-3873).

California

National Forests in California

Angeles National Forest, 150 South Los Robles, Suite 300, Pasadena, CA 91101 (213-577-0050).

Cleveland National Forest, 880 Front St., Sand Diego, CA 92188 (619-293-5050).

Eldorado National Forest, 100 Forni Rd., Placerville, CA 95667 (916-622-5061).

Inyo National Forest, 873 North Main St., Bishop, CA 93414 (619-873-5841).

Klamath National Forest, 1312 Fairland Rd., Yreka, CA 96097 (916-842-6131).

Lassen National Forest, 707 Nevada St., Susanville, CA 96130 (916-257-2151).

Los Padres National Forest, 42 Aero Camino, Goleta, CA 93117 (805-968-1578).

Mendocino National Forest, 420 E. Laurel St., Willows, CA 95988 (916-934-3316).

Modoc National Forest, 441 N. Main St., Alturas, CA 96101 (916-233-5811).

Plumas National Forest, 159 Lawrence St., Box 1500, Quincy, CA 95971 (916-283-2050).

San Bernardino National Forest, 144 N. Mountain View, San Bernardino, CA 92408 (714-383-5588).

Sequoia National Forest, 900 W. Grand Ave., Porterville, CA 93257 (209-784-1500).

Shasta-Trinity National Forest, 2400 Washington Ave., Redding, CA 96001 (916-246-5222).

Sierra National Forest, Federal Bldg., 1130 O St., Room 3017, Fresno, CA 93721 (209-487-5155).

Six Rivers National Forest, 507 F St., Eureka, CA 95501 (707-442-1721).

Stanislaus National Forest, 19777 Greenley Rd., Sonora, CA 95370 (209-532-3671).

Tahoe National Forest, Highway 49, Nevada City, CA 95959 (916-265-4531).

Bureau of Land Management: California State Office, Federal Office Bldg., Rm. E-2841, 2800 Cottage Way, Sacramento, CA 95825 (916-484-4676).

Colorado

National Forests in Colorado

Arapho and Roosevelt National Forests, Federal Bldg., 301 S. Howes, Fort Collins, CO 80521 (303-482-5155).

Grand Mesa, Uncompahgre, and Gunnison National Forests, 11th and Main St., P.O. Box 138, Delta, CO 81416 (303-874-7691).

Pike and San Isabel National Forests, 910 Highway 50 West, Pueblo, CO 81008 (303-544-5277).

Rio Grande National Forest, 1803 W. Highway 160, Monte Vista, CO 81144 (303-852-5941).

Routt National Forest, Hunt Bldg., Steamboat Springs, CO 80477 (303-897-1722).

San Juan National Forest, Federal Bldg., 701 Caminoo Del Rio, Durango, CO 81301 (303-247-4874).

White River National Forest, Old Federal Building, Box 948, Glenwood Springs, CO 81601 (303-945-6582).

Bureau of Land Management: Colorado State Office, Colorado State Bank Building, 1600 Broadway, Denver, CO 80202 (303-837-4325).

Idaho

National Forests in Idaho

Boise National Forest, 1075 Park Blvd., Boise, ID 83706 (208-334-1516).

Caribou National Forest, 250 S. Fourth Ave., Pocatello, ID 83201 (208-232-1142).

Challis National Forest, Forest Service Bldg., Challis, ID 83226 (208-879-2285).

Clearwater National Forest, Rt. 4, Orofino, ID 83544 (208-476-4541).

Idaho Panhandle National Forest, 1201 Ironwood Drive, Couer d'Alene, ID 83814 (208-667-2561).

Nezperce National Forest, 319 E. Main St., Grangeville, ID 83530 (208-983-1950).

Payette National Forest, Forest Service Bldg., P.O. Box 1026, McCall, ID 83638 (208-634-2255).

Salmon National Forest, Forest Service Bldg., Salmon, ID 83467 (208-756-2215).

Sawtooth National Forest, 1525 Addison Ave. East, Twin Falls, ID 83301 (208-733-3698).

Targhee National Forest, 420 N. Bridge St., St. Anthony, ID 83455 (208-624-3151).

Bureau of Land Management: Idaho State Office, 398 Federal Bldg., 550 W. Fort St., Boise, ID 83724 (208-384-1401).

Montana

National Forests in Montana

Beaverhead National Forest, P.O. Box 1258, Dillon, MT 59725 (406-683-2312).

Bitterroot National Forest, 316 N. Third St., Hamilton, MT 59840 (406-363-3131).

Custer National Forest, P.O. Box 2556, Billings, MT 59103 (406-657-6361).

Deerlodge National Forest, Federal Bldg., P.O. Box 400, Butte, MT 59701 (406-723-6561).

Flathead National Forest, P.O. Box 147, 290 N. Main, Kalispell, MT 59901 (406-755-5401).

Gallatin National Forest, Federal Bldg., P.O. Box 130, Bozeman, MT 59715 (406-587-5271).

Helena National Forest, Federal Bldg., Drawer 10014, Helena, MT 59601 (406-449-5201).

Kootenai National Forest, W. Highway 2, Libby, MT 59923 (406-293-6211).

Lewis and Clark National Forest, Federal Bldg., Great Falls, MT 59403 (406-453-7678).

Bureau of Land Management: Montana State Office, 222 N. 32nd St., P.O. Box 30157, Billings, MT 59107 (406-657-6462).

Nevada

National Forests in Nevada

Humboldt National Forest, 976 Mountain City Highway, Elko, NV 89801 (702-738-5171).

Toiyabe National Forest, 111 N. Virginia St., Room 601, Reno, NV 89501 (702-784-5331).

Bureau of Land Management: Nevada State Office, Federal Bldg., Rm. 3008, 300 Booth St., Reno, NV 89520 (702-784-5451).

New Mexico

National Forests in New Mexico

Carson National Forest, Forest Service Bldg., P.O. Box 558, Taos, NM 87571 (505-758-2238).

Cibola National Forest, 10308 Candelaria NE, Albuquerque, NM 87112 (505-766-2185).

Gila National Forest, 2610 N. Silver St., Silver City, NM 88061 (505-388-1986).

Lincoln National Forest, Federal Bldg., 11th and New York, Alamogordo, NM 88310 (505-437-6030).

Santa Fe National Forest, Federal Bldg., Box 1689, Santa Fe, NM 87501 (505-988-6328).

Bureau of Land Management: New Mexico State Office, Federal Bldg., South Federal Place, Santa Fe, NM 87501 (505-988-6217).

Oregon

National Forests in Oregon

Deschutes National Forest, 211 NE Revere Ave., Bend, OR 97701 (503-382-6922).

Fremont National Forest, 34 North D St., Lakeview, OR 97630 (503-947-2151).

Malheur National Forest, 139 NE Dayton St., John Day, OR 97845 (503-575-1731).

Mt. Hood National Forest, 2440 SE 195th, Portland, OR 97233 (503-667-0511).

Ochoco National Forest, Federal Bldg., Prineville, OR 97754 (503-447-6247).

Rogue River National Forest, Federal Bldg., 333 W. Eighth St., P.O. Box 520, Medford, OR 97501 (503-779-2351).

Siskiyou National Forest, P.O. Box 440, Grants Pass, OR 97526 (503-479-5301).

Siuslaw National Forest, P.O. Box 1148, Corvallis, OR 97330 (503-757-4480).

Umatilla National Forest, 2517 SW Hailey Ave., Pendleton, OR 97801 (503-276-3811).

Umpqua National Forest, Federal Office Bldg., Roseburg, OR 97470 (503-672-6601).

Wallawa and Whitman National Forests, Federal Office Bldg., P.O. Box 907, Baker, OR 97814 (503-523-6391).

Willamette National Forest, 211 E. Seventh Ave., Eugene, OR 97440 (503-687-6533).

Winema National Forest, P.O. Box 1390, Klamath Falls, OR 97601 (503-882-7761).

Bureau of Land Management: 729 NE Oregon St., P.O. Box 2965, Portland, OR 97208 (503-234-4001).

Utah

National Forests in Utah

Ashley National Forest, 437 E. Main St., Vernal, UT 84078 (801-789-1181).

Dixie National Forest, 82 N. 100 E. St., Cedar City, UT 84720 (801-586-2421).

Fishlake National Forest, 170 N. Main St., Richfield, UT 84701 (801-896-4491).

Manti-Lasal National Forest, 599 West 100 South, Price, UT 84501 (801-637-2817).

Uinta National Forest, 88 West 1 North, Provo, UT 84601 (801-584-9101).

Wasatch National Forest, 8226 Federal Bldg., 125 South State St., Salt Lake City, UT 84138 (801-524-5030).

Bureau of Land Management: Utah State Office, University Club Bldg., 136 South Temple, Salt Lake City, UT 84111 (801-524-5311).

Washington

National Forests in Washington

Colville National Forest, Colville, WA 99114 (509-684-5221).

Gifford Pinchot National Forest, 500 W. 12th St., Vancouver, WA 98660 (206-696-4041).

Mt. Baker and Snoqualmie National Forests, 1601 Second Ave., Seattle, WA 98101 (206-442-5400).

Okanogan National Forest, 1240 Second Ave. S., Okanogan, WA 98840 (509-422-2704).

Olympia National Forest, P.O. Box 2288, Olympia, WA 98507 (206-753-9534).

Wenatchee National Forest, 301 Yakima St., Wenatchee, WA 98801 (509-662-4323).

Bureau of Land Management: 729 NE Oregon St., P.O. Box 2965, Portland, OR 97208 (503-234-4001).

Wyoming

National Forests in Wyoming

Bridger-Teton National Forest, Forest Service Bldg., Jackson, WY 83001 (307-733-2752).

Bighorn National Forest, Columbus Bldg., P.O. Box 2046, Sheridan, WY 82801 (307-672-2457).

Medicine Bow National Forest, 605 Skyline Dr., Laramie, WY 82070 (307-745-8971).

Shoshone National Forest, West Yellowstone Highway, P.O. Box 2140, Cody, WY 82414 (307-587-2274).

Bureau of Land Management: Wyoming State Office, 2515 Warren Ave., P.O. Box 1828, Cheyenne, WY 82001 (307-778-2326).

Some other fine books for hunters
from America's Great Outdoor Publisher

Badge in the Wilderness
My 30 dangerous years combating wildlife violators.
by David H. Swendsen

Grouse Hunter's Guide
Solid facts, insights, and observations on how to hunt the ruffed grouse.
by Dennis Walrod

Microwave Game & Fish Cookbook
Quick, convenient recipes for concocting the tastiest, juiciest, most succulent wild meat
and fish meals you've ever eaten.
by Paula J. Del Guidice

Wildlife Management on Your Land
The practical owner's manual on how, what, when, and why.
by Charles L. Cadieux

White-tailed Deer: Ecology & Management
Developed by the Wildlife Management Institute. Over 2,400 references on every aspect
of deer behavior.
edited by Lowell K. Halls

Bowhunting for Whitetails
Your best methods for taking North America's favorite deer.
by Dave Bowring

Deer & Deer Hunting
The serious hunter's guide.
by Dr. Rob Wegner

Elk of North America
The definitive, exhaustive, classic work on the North American elk. Developed by the
Wildlife Management Institute.
ed. by Jack Ward Thomas and Dale E. Toweill

Hunting Ducks and Geese
Hard facts, good bets, and serious advice from a duck hunter you can trust.
by Steve Smith

Bear Hunting
First complete guide on the how-tos of bear hunting.
by Jerry Meyer

Sylvia Bashline's Savory Game Cookbook
150 recipes and complete instructions for enhancing the unique natural flavors of game-
birds, waterfowl, big and small-game meats.
by Sylvia Bashline

Art and Science of Whitetail Hunting
How to Interpret the Facts and Find the Deer.
by Kent Horner

Available at your local bookstore, or
for complete ordering information, write:

Stackpole Books
Dept. WH
Cameron and Kelker Streets
Harrisburg, PA 17105

For fast service credit card users may call 1-800-READ-NOW.
In Pennsylvania, call 717-234-5041